Canterbury
History You Can See

Canterbury
History You Can See

Marjorie Lyle

In gratitude to many citizens of Canterbury who helped me over half a century.

First published in 2008
Reprinted in 2009, 2013

The History Press
The Mill, Brimscombe Port,
Stroud, Gloucestershire, GL5 2QG
www.thehistorypress.co.uk

© Marjorie Lyle, 2008

The right of Marjorie Lyle to be identified as the Author
of this work has been asserted in accordance with the
Copyrights, Designs and Patents Act 1988.

All rights reserved. No part of this book may be reprinted
or reproduced or utilised in any form or by any electronic,
mechanical or other means, now known or hereafter invented,
including photocopying and recording, or in any information
storage or retrieval system, without the permission in writing
from the Publishers.

British Library Cataloguing in Publication Data.
A catalogue record for this book is available from the British Library.

ISBN 978 0 7524 4538 0

Typesetting and origination by
The History Press
Printed in Great Britain

Contents

	Foreword	7
	Introduction	10
one	The World Heritage Site	11
two	The Blackfriars Quarter	34
three	Outside the Western Walls	51
four	The Greyfriars Quarter	66
five	The Whitefriars Quarter	93
six	Outside the Eastern Walls	115
	Further Reading	126

CANTERBURY: THE HISTORY YOU CAN SEE

WH World Heritage Site
W   Canterbury West Railway Station
E   Canterbury East Railway Station
B   Bus Station

Blackfriars   Chapter 2
Greyfriars   Chapter 4
Whitefriars   Chapter 5

Foreword

I am very grateful to all the bodies and individuals who, while retaining their copyrights, have given me permission to use their images. If I have omitted any person or image please accept my apologies: The Dean and Chapter of Canterbury Cathedral; Canterbury City Council; Canterbury Archaeological Trust Ltd.; Canterbury Commemoration Society and Don Grant; Canterbury Royal Museums; St Edmund's School; The Trustees of the Eastbridge Hospital; Paul Crampton; Ken Kashian; John Kemp; Revd. Pamela Lloyd; Kenneth Pinnock; Revd. Maurice Worgan.

John Kemp not only took and processed many extra photographs but spent hours leading us through computer imaging. Without him this book would not have reached the publishers. I also thank Stewart Ross and Andrew Savage for their technical assistance. I am indebted to John Hills of Canterbury Christ Church University who designed the maps. Other images were our own or came from the collection of the late Canon Derek Ingram Hill.

This book is as much the creation of my patient husband Lawrence and his computer as of me; I now owe him a debt of fifty-eight years of loving support.

Aerial view. The Roman and medieval walls encircle a town dominated by the Cathedral and Precincts on the site of the Saxon stronghold. The 1960-1990 modern buildings occupy the main area of bomb-damage in 1942, now again rebuilt.

Introduction

Have you ever come home from a day trip to a place like Canterbury feeling punch-drunk? Sometimes there is too much history to see. Great buildings like cathedrals can dwarf their neighbours and smother the memory of their various builders. City walls, seventeen centuries old, hide the changes which altered them. Yet every building which has survived war, slump, plague and changing fashion was adapted to new uses and can reveal its story and the lives of its inhabitants high and low.

I hope to introduce you to the builders, traders, craftsmen, scholars, saints and sinners who created and lived in Canterbury during its long history by looking at all its buildings, as well as its great World Heritage Site.

Cities, like plants and people, sometimes grow quickly, sometimes stand still and occasionally have to adapt to disaster. Just as you read a tree's history from its rings, a city's history can be read from its buildings as well as from objects and documents their owners left behind.

People have lived, worked and died here at the Stour crossing for over 2,000 years; for half that time, as the chief Christian centre of England, Canterbury's history was part of the nation's history. Five archbishops lived and died for great issues of Church and State. St Augustine left his footprint at St Martin's, his abbey and at the Cathedral; St Alphege tried to defend the city from the Danes; St Thomas' murder in 1170 founded and still sustains the city's fortunes. Thomas Cranmer, burnt under Mary Tudor, and William Laud, executed during the Civil War, left us Anglican liturgy and forms of worship.

Little remains above ground of the first two building booms because the Roman city, which fell into decay in the fifth century, became the stone quarry for Saxons and Normans. The Saxon town, damaged by the Vikings in the 800s, was sacked again in 1011. Much of what we see today comes from two great bursts of medieval building in the 1100-1200s and again after the Black Death from 1380.

Canterbury's greatest challenge came when Henry VIII, after his breach with Rome, closed the religious houses and destroyed the shrine of St Thomas Becket. A century of religious strife and civil war would follow.

The eighteenth-century market town saw a new phase of destructive modernisation and building with the arrival of the coaching trade and the regiments. There are a few elegant Georgian survivals here but much was lost during the German air raids of the war years. Post-war clearance and rebuilding was often hasty and ugly. The arrival of the universities and modern tourism have heralded a new burst of development, tempered since 1974 by new attitudes to historic city conservation by national and local government.

We must be grateful that in the Victorian era the sleepy cathedral market town had little incentive to pull down, rebuild or expand since industry largely passed it by. Vigilance is needed today to protect the complete townscape of big and little houses and shops which this quiet time left behind. For the new wave of developers, like their medieval and Georgian counterparts, want the city to adapt lest it perish. If a proper balance is struck between the impact of traffic and tourism and the needs of residents the city should survive the next millennium.

one
The World Heritage Site

St Martin's Church: The Arrival of Christianity to the Anglo-Saxons

Below the brow of a hill about half-a-mile from Canterbury, on the Roman road to Richborough Fort, a little building probably began as a pagan shrine. It was later adapted as an occasional Church by Roman Christians, who usually worshipped at home. Some of the silver they would have used, bearing Christian symbols, was buried by a silversmith near the Westgate in dangerous days about AD 410. It is now displayed in the Roman Museum.

One-hundred-and-fifty years later, King Ethelbert concluded a political marriage contract with Charibert, king in Paris, whose Christian daughter Bertha successfully begged for her chaplain Liudhart to accompany her to pagan Kent. The two would trudge from the King's hall through the old Roman postern gate now called Queningate, embedded in the city wall in the Broad Street car park, to the then ruinous chapel. This they rebuilt, dedicating it to Martin, patron saint of Tours, where Bertha had grown up. The south wall of the chancel, of solid Roman brickwork, contains a small Saxon door; outside it the Victorians found a little medal bearing Liudhart's name.

After some years of Bertha's gentle persuasion, Ethelbert admitted St Augustine's mission of AD 597, giving them St Martin's as their first base. After his baptism and the founding of an abbey and cathedral, this church became the centre of a thriving suburb and needed expanding. The present nave dates mainly from the 600s, built by the monks to the pattern of the churches they had left behind in Rome. Its flint and reused Roman brick walls also contain French Marquise stone, perhaps acquired by Queen Bertha.

Despite the additions and alterations of fourteen centuries it remains today England's oldest continually used church, with a view from the churchyard of all the first three Christian buildings of the mission sent by Pope Gregory. The Victorians thought that the unusual font was where Ethelbert was baptised; he and his noble entourage were more probably baptised in the river Stour. The font is late Saxon in the lower two tiers and features as a wellhead in Prior Wibert's famous diagram of his cathedral priory water system of the 1160s. When it was brought here as a font the Norman arcaded top tier was presumably added to heighten it; you can see where a crude insertion was made to refit the rim.

When the perpendicular tower was added, the west wall was clearly altered by blocking early windows, altering the doorway and changing the roof line. As you leave through the tower spare a thought for Speaker Finch of the House of Commons whose monument adorns the north wall. In 1629 he was held down in his chair while the 'Petition of Right' was voted through the Commons; Charles I then closed parliament for eleven years. Finch remained a Royalist, going into exile during the Commonwealth. Returning in 1660, he tried the regicides who had voted for the King's execution and died soon afterwards.

St Martin's is the first part of our World Heritage Site. In 2006 Prince Michael of Kent and the French Consul-General unveiled Stephen Melton's striking statues outside St Augustine's Abbey Gate. Ethelbert is greeting his queen on her return from St Martin's Church.

Above: The south wall of St Martin's Church. Queen Bertha's square-headed door and a later Saxon door puncture a largely intact Roman wall of the ruinous chapel she restored before 597. Afterwards the church was extended leftwards still using Roman brick from the nearby cemetery. Part of the original porch is embedded in the buttress.

Left: St Martin's Church font. The adapted well-head transported from the Cathedral is described here.

Opposite: Queen Bertha at Fyndon Gate. This French queen died before Ethelbert and was buried in St Augustine's Abbey. Their son King Eadbald briefly reverted to paganism and built a second church on the Abbey site in penitence. (See the cover for the companion Ethelbert statue by Stephen Melton.)

Wulfric's Rotunda. The late Saxon rotunda was planned to unite the first two churches. It was buried beneath the Norman rebuild which in turn was destroyed on Henry VIII's orders in 1538. Gradually excavated by members of the Victorian missionary college, the site has been under national guardianship since 1910.

St Augustine's Abbey: where to put the monks?

You might ask why these piles of old stones, however well-preserved and explained by English Heritage, should form the second part of Canterbury's World Heritage Site.

There are three good reasons from the formative Saxon centuries which have left behind very little 'history you can see'.

First, more than half the missionary party were monks, not priests, and so unable to say Mass, consecrate churches or ordain others. The monks' role was to maintain the ceaseless round of prayer, educate young noblemen and build a fitting mausoleum for archbishops and kings of Kent to become a magnet for pilgrims. King Ethelbert gave them the old Roman cemetery outside the walls for their abbey. You can see the burial place of the first five archbishops and traces of their first churches, all in the form of a square nave, with porch and annexes and probably a shallow apse. All these remains contain much Roman brick from the old cemetery best seen at St Pancras, the most easterly site.

Next, it was here that the Greek academic from Tarsus, Archbishop Theodore with his friend Abbot Hadrian, set up a school in the 670s attracting scholars from all over western

Christendom. He was described as 'a wild boar, beset by Irish wolf-hounds, repelling them with the sharp tooth of his logic'. One pupil, Albinus, became abbot here and was Bede's chief source when writing his *Ecclesiastical History* of the conversion story. Theodore's example of a Canterbury university proved powerful in later centuries (see pp 45, 64 and 119). It is fitting that Christ Church, one of our two universities, is sited on abbey ground today.

Thirdly, this was the only abbey in Kent to escape sacking by the Vikings in the late 800s. St Dunstan rededicated the expanded abbey, adding St Augustine's name to SS Peter and Paul by which it had been known. It became such a famous centre for scholarship and illumination that in 1011 Abbot Aelfmar, knowing its exposed position outside the city walls, seems to have done a deal with Thorkell the Tall and Olaf the Stout when Vikings returned to besiege and capture Canterbury, enslave its people and later murder Archbishop Alphege.

The abbey's fame for beautiful manuscripts blossomed until the Norman Conquest. Only a precious 150 manuscripts survive today from Henry VIII's dissolution of 1538. However, among Pope Gregory's books sent in 601 is the *Canterbury Gospels*, held in Cambridge, on which each new Archbishop takes his oath at his enthronement.

What you can see on site is **Abbot Wulfric's** attempt to link the two earliest churches of the 600s by a **rotunda of the 1040s**. Unfinished in 1066 it prompted the new Norman Abbot Scolland to scrap the lot and rebuild in imported Caen stone, using all the Saxon material as rubble core. He got papal permission to shift the early archbishops' bones to magnificent new shrines round the high altar in an abbey church rivalling the cathedral in size. Buttressed by income from extensive land-grants throughout Kent, building in the church and monastic buildings continued to the final years, when the Lady chapel was erected.

Again, almost nothing survived the thorough demolition by Henry VIII's commissioner, James Needham. After stone had been carted off to Calais and Henry's coastal castles, more was sold off to the citizens at eight pence a cartload (see page 106). Only the north nave wall stands today, supporting the Tudor brickwork of Henry's Royal Palace (see colour plate 5).

English Heritage's excellent audio-guides at several levels allow for a full exploration of all the phases of this large site. The ruins are enlivened in the summer by open-air theatrical performances, occasional sound and light shows and children's events.

The Cathedral

This third part of the World Heritage Site has so much to see inside and out that in fifty years I have not exhausted its surprises.

Where was it?

Before 1993 nobody knew exactly where the first cathedral lay. Bede tells how Ethelbert gave a Roman ruin to St Augustine for the purpose and scholars discounted the memories of Eadmer writing as an old monk of the Saxon cathedral of his youth. Archaeologists expected little of a dig limited in time and dimension when the nave floor of 1788 was being renewed. Removing rubble from a looted medieval grave at the east end of the nave where Eadmer had located the monks' choir, the archaeologists revealed a stratification. Two Roman levels underlay the black earth of abandonment; bedded into the top of this layer were reused Roman brick foundations. Further traces of a small square church akin to those at St Augustine's were found and seem to be of the 600s. Today **the Compass Rose** symbolizing the spread of the Anglican Church worldwide lies over the probable site of the Roman mission's early cathedral which remained the monks' choir until 1130.

Opposite: The Compass Rose. This symbol of the spread of the Anglican Communion, lying over the probable site of the Roman missionaries' first cathedral of 598, has become the focal point for special services.

Norman floor. The Lanfranc floor of 1077, pitted with medieval graves, still supported the fourteenth-century Perpendicular piers and were found below the floor of 1788 during the third repaving in 1993.

Another spectacular discovery was the great western apse of the eleventh century which made the Saxon cathedral England's largest stone building. The wartime fire-watchers' memorial indicates its position today.

Two Norman builders
In 1070, Lanfranc, the reluctant elderly Italian scholar from France, was consecrated archbishop in a wooden hut within the burnt-out nave. In seven years he and Prior Gundulf, called over from their joint work at St Etienne, Caen, would rebuild it, determining its size, location and two western towers. In 1077 Gundulf was released to become Bishop of Rochester. There he began to build the castle and cathedral on the banks of the Medway and designed the White Tower on the Thames for William the Conqueror. The nave was moved 10m southward to create a larger cloister for the 150 monks Lanfranc hoped would regenerate the English Church. His solid floor, we discovered, still supports the fifteenth-century columns of the nave today. His four crossing pillars, filled with rubble from the Roman theatre, still support the weight of Bell Harry Tower

Above: The Quire. Looking eastwards to the Corona this view encompasses the work of English William, tapering within the Romanseque shell left from th e fire of 1174.

Left: The Romanesque shell. Within this cleared space William of Sens began his Gothic work in 1175-76. This earlier work 1is what you see walking round outside.

which would later replace his shorter structure. Despite a heavy workload as the conqueror's 'number two' he remained until eighty-one a compulsive builder (see pp 26 and 29).

Go for Gothic

Beating their fists against the burnt stones the monks lamented the disastrous fire of 1174 which destroyed their Romanesque quire where Becket had ministered only four years earlier. Amazingly they chose a pioneer of the Gothic style, William from Sens, who promised a quire, ambulatories, presbytery and a new Trinity chapel for Becket's shrine, all within the standing Romanesque shell. Gervase the monk left us a yearly description of how the work proceeded eastwards, increasingly Gothic, the first for England, up to William's dramatic fall while supervising the installation of a keystone. After three months on a stretcher he left for France, leaving his trained successor, William the Englishman, to carry on the transformation towards the Corona and below in the Eastern Crypt where Becket's body still lay.

Thanks to politics under King John, only in July 1220 could Archbishop Stephen Langton preside over the 'translation' of Becket's relics to his new shrine. The good and great from young King Henry III downwards were there. Henceforward this July event shared the honours with the December murder, doubling pilgrim numbers and offerings. The great strip cartoons showing the miracles wrought, which still fill most windows round the Trinity Chapel with thirteenth-century glass, were but part of the Becket cult (colour plate 2). The Corona was a pun for there, within its crown shape, the sliced crown of the saint's head, which won him a martyr's crown, lay in its reliquary. In time the tombs of Henry IV and the Black Prince would flank the shrine but every pilgrim went home stunned by this Gothic novelty saying 'We must have Gothic too'. From Chichester to Lincoln the style's popularity spread and in time, under the Victorian revival, would reach the antipodes.

Rebuilding the nave

The vertical and diagonal vistas of Canterbury's nave, flooded with light from 40ft windows, combine with its marvellous lierne vaulting into one of the most beautiful spaces created in mediaeval England (colour plate 1). Yet it went up during thirty turbulent years which saw the Peasants' Revolt and a change of dynasty punctuated by a severe earthquake. Two kings and three archbishops contributed handsomely but the masterminds behind the two phases were Henry Yevele and Prior Thomas Chillenden.

The Gothic east end's symbolic impact had been the successive steps by which pilgrims ascended from the nave level to Becket's shrine. Yet when, after the Black Prince's state funeral in 1376, it was decided to rebuild the small, shabby, Romanesque nave, it was also decided that the high eastern roofline should be continued to the west at the same level. So, although Lanfranc's nave was limited in length by its western towers, only the architect's daring limited how high it could soar towards the new roof.

In 1377 Archbishop Simon Sudbury, the chancellor who would afterwards be blamed for the Poll Tax and murdered by Wat Tyler's rebels, generously paid over £2,000 to demolish the old nave and rebuild the side aisles with their vast Perpendicular windows. His arms adorn some bosses there. Payments are recorded to Henry Yevele (see page 31), the King's master-mason, who had been building the Black Prince's crypt chantry and was also designing a new nave for Westminster Abbey. Until his death in 1400 he was occupied too on Canterbury's Westgate and city walls. Colleagues on the spot like Stephen Lote would often supervise this busy man's plans.

Work proceeded apace up to 1382, aided by Richard II whose arms appear on it. Then the severe earthquake so damaged the adjoining cloister area that only £400 was spent on the nave in the next nine years. When Thomas Chillenden, 'the greatest builder of a Prior that ever was', took over in 1391 he galvanized the second phase. He managed the monastic estates so profitably that he could spend £3,000 over the next six years, augmented by Archbishop Courtenay's contributions.

Richard II's deposition by Henry IV brought in two new patrons by 1400, his Archbishop Arundel and the King himself. Devoted to St Thomas and planning his own tomb here, the contributions of King, courtiers and Prince Hal are recorded in arms on the western works. The huge west window, today containing the oldest glass, was glazed by 1398 and all was finished by 1405. The aisle vaults were only a foot shorter than the 50ft slender piers supporting the screen walls which hid the monks' upper walkway. They then soared up past the clerestory to the intricate lierne vaulting 80ft above the floor.

This could not be the end, for the central and south-western towers had been so disturbed that more successful fund-raising was needed from both Yorkist and Tudor regimes under Chillenden's successors.

More history to see in the nave is the Laudian font of 1639, dismantled by Puritan iconoclasts, rescued and hidden by the antiquarian Somner to be used for his son's baptism after the Restoration. Among the wall monuments are those to the composer Orlando Gibbons, soldiers of the 1842 Afghan War and Lieutenant Bennett, killed in a local wood while suppressing the last agricultural revolt of 1838 (see page 91).

Bell Harry Tower: The Brilliant Afterthought

In 1433 the first stone was laid of a new 'Angel Steeple' to replace Lanfranc's squat tower topped with a spire and angel figure. Even starting this work involved recasing Lanfranc's piers. Twenty years later further strengthening was needed, seemingly prompting the decision to employ lighter bricks inside the stone façades of the lantern tower. The Wars of the Roses depleted funds and removed workmen. Only in 1477 were new 'redde bryks' ordered to complete the proposed bell-tower above the lantern level, meant to hold the 'Bell Harry' called after an earlier prior (see page 30).

The new player, when the wars ended with Henry VII's accession, was his friend and notoriously successful money-extracting chancellor, John Morton, whom he made archbishop in 1486. Achieving his cardinal's cap in 1493 he decided to 'cap' his cathedral and introduced his own architect John Wastell to Prior Sellinge, the administrator on the spot.

How to erect a 235ft tower, 100ft of it above the roof level, on apparently unstable twelfth-century piers, while recasting the exterior of the existing tower to harmonise was a huge engineering and design problem. Wastell solved it magnificently between 1494 and 1503 aided by Sellinge who fed in 440,000 bricks, relays of Caen stone in 39-ton lots and paid the masons at £8/ft.

When you observe the tower outside you can see how he lightened the load with huge windows, scooped-out corner buttresses, pierced parapets and eye-deceiving tall pinnacles giving the impression of greater height still. You cannot see either the quantity of light brick inside or the plethora of Morton's arms and cardinal's cap adorning the upper parts. Inside, you can see the cunningly inserted decorative strainer arches which bind Lanfranc's four pillars together. You forget them when looking up into the lantern's fan vaulting, the precursor in 1509 of Wastell's King's College Chapel, Cambridge. Canterbury would propel his career there and in Peterborough and Bury St Edmunds.

Not only is the tower of surpassing beauty but it fittingly links the French and English Gothic of east and west and in its detailed written story reveals the process and costing of these huge, lengthy mediaeval building projects.

The Bell Harry wheel. This fifteenth-century building aid for hauling up stone and brick remains *in situ*. Canon Hill standing in it knew, loved and described the Cathedral for over seventy years.

The Crypt. The chapel of Our Lady Undercroft is an oasis of quiet and prayer in this oldest part of the Cathedral.

The Crypt: The Underground Story

The Saxon cathedral had contained a sunken shrine to St Dunstan, replaced by the short crypt under Lanfranc's east end; the only vestige of his work is the rear wall of today's treasury. Early in the 1100s the Romanesque western crypt was created to support Conrad's great quire existing in Becket's day and burnt in 1174. Twenty-two columns bear axe-hewn designs where carved columns alternate with carved capitals. The former seemingly arrived precarved; the latter to have been worked in place in fanciful designs of lions and jugglers with barely Christian significance, perhaps by Saxon carvers. 'Green' lions and cats, foliage in mouth, adorn several crypt capitals and a Green Man appears in the Huguenot chapel, whilst five more hide in the cloister walls by the Martyrdom door. In St Gabriel's side chapel another half-human, wrestling with dragons, accompanies early Christian wall paintings.

The Chapel of Our Lady Undercroft, a quiet place for prayer, is enclosed by fourteenth-century screens. It was a favourite with the Black Prince and where he hoped to be buried, but the tomb to the right is Cardinal Morton's of Bell Harry fame. The Prince's chantry in the nearby side chapel, redesigned by Yevele, is still the French Protestant Church holding weekly services. The whole crypt was given by Queen Elizabeth I to the first 100 refugee weaver families from France and Belgium in 1575 to be their church, school and court for running their own affairs. Worshippers above would frequently complain of their loud French singing.

When in 1170 Becket's enemy de Broc threatened to drag his body to feed the pigs the monks hid it behind Our Lady's altar at the end of the original apse. However, the extension of the Gothic work eastwards by English William needed a crypt extension too. Two massive pillars support the quire above but beyond lies a dramatic demonstration of the revolutionary move from Romanesque to Gothic.

Above: When damp threatened the surviving frescoes in St Gabriel's chapel excavations during repair work revealed a pagan Roman shrine with votive offerings with which this semi-pagan human figure eight centuries later has some affinity.

Right: The door of the Martyrdom. The modern cross, formed to represent the knights' swords, marks the site of the Altar of the Sword Point where the broken tip of Le Bret's sword was preserved until the Reformation.

For fifty years to 1220 Becket's body would lie here in the eastern crypt, his lead-covered coffin encased in marble with oval apertures for pilgrims to touch. Two thin Purbeck marble columns flank the spot, supporting the roof over increasingly pointed arches. The ambulatory allowed pilgrims to circulate, observed from the windows of the watching chamber above by two monks, Benedict and William, who recorded the early miracle stories. These are portrayed in the miracle windows round the later shrine and show the original appearance of the tomb.

The Jesus Chapel with its sixteenth-century painted ceiling lies below the Corona and concludes the east end. The King's School now uses the eastern crypt for their services.

The Martyrdom

The name of Thomas Becket has appeared at intervals throughout this description of the cathedral's parts. It has become clear that most of what we see today arose from the shockingly dramatic story of his murder and the consequent astounding transformation of the fortunes of the monks who, in life, had often resented and distrusted him.

This is no place to describe either the motivation of the four knights or the long struggle between Thomas, defending the rights and liberties of the Church, from the way his old friend Henry II was trying to restore the King's writ and the rule of law after the Anarchy of Stephen's reign. After six years' exile he had returned to his cathedral and priory in December 1170 to a huge backlog of disputes. The earlier events of the afternoon of Tuesday 29 December are described at Conquest House (see page 39) but we now stand in the north-west transept known as the Martyrdom, surveying the door to the cloisters on which so much hinges. As his procession entered for vespers, Thomas' order to leave the door unbarred implicitly accepted that, although God was able to spare him, if not 'His will be done'. The knights burst in through the door demanding 'Where is Thomas Becket, traitor to the King?' plainly hoping to drag him out of sanctuary into the cloisters. Given Becket's height and strength, his provocative remarks to FitzUrse and their failure to get him on to de Tracy's back, he was struck down in the heat of the moment by three successive blows to the head. However, this was not before he had called on St Alphege, the first martyred archbishop, and had fallen facing the altar of St Benedict, the father of monasticism. 'Come, knights, this one's not rising again!' cried Hugh Mauclerc who had shown them the way and out to the cloister they ran shouting 'King's men!'

In the interval before his valet arrived from the palace or the monks returned with a stretcher, the crowd awaiting their vespers, no longer held back by de Moreville, clustered like ants round the corpse, gathering brains and blood-soaked rags. One of these produced the first alleged miracle on Agnes, a blind woman, that same evening. The snowballing of popular acclaim, together with the monks' discovery of Becket's monastic habit and lice-ridden hair garments beneath his robes fuelled the horror at this sacrilegious murder. Recorded by five eye-witnesses, this became the best-documented event in medieval England.

The original appearance of the Martyrdom was later altered by the Altar of the Sword Point where he fell, by architectural changes following the building of the new quire, by burials and by the replacement of the old Chapels of St Benedict with St Blaise above by the Dean's fan-vaulted chapel. To see Pope John Paul II and Archbishop Runcie kneeling together on this spot was very moving (see colour plate 5). Afterwards they both lit candles for today's martyrs at the Corona where Thomas' severed skull once rested in its reliquary. Every 29 December sees a procession to the Martyrdom led by the Archbishop.

Stephen Langton's tomb. This part of Archbishop Langton's tomb is not visible today below the altar of the Buffs' Chapel largely filled by the later vast table tomb of Lady Margaret Holland and her husbands.

The Precincts
This area is occupied by private properties round which we walk by permission.

Leaving the cathedral by the south-west door you cross the deep porch finished in 1418 to commemorate Henry V's victory at Agincourt. The arms of the King, his friend Archbishop Chichele and sixteen warrior nobles adorn the vaulting, for Henry himself attended a celebratory mass here on his way home. Its exterior shows the Altar of the Sword Point which stood in the Martyrdom; the empty niches probably held depictions of Becket's murder but all the statuary fell to puritan vandals in 1642-43. Inspired by St Peter's in Rome, Dean Alford in the 1850s aimed to make the cathedral an equally inspiring centre of the Anglican Church. He employed the Belgian sculptor Pfyffers to carve St Augustine, Ethelbert and Bertha for the porch, other historic and Victorian worthies for the west end and began the rolling repair programme which still brings scaffolding to any part of the fabric today.

Until 1814 this south side was the site of the three-day Michaelmas Fair, a hiring fair with exciting sideshows. The monastic buildings lay unusually on the quieter northern side. To reach them, moving anticlockwise you pass the foot of Stephen Langton's coffin projecting eastwards from the chapel to the right of the smaller south door. Lady Margaret Holland's tomb, flanked by her two royal husbands, involved a rebuilding of the chapel which left this great archbishop's feet in the cold. Yet he had compelled King John to seal Magna Carta in 1215. **The International Study Centre** (Whitfield Associates) was the project of Dean Simpson, opened in 2000-01, with auditorium, education centre and residential accommodation for visiting conferences. It replaced houses developed on the campanile site after the New Foundation of 1542. As you walk past the entrance to the French Chapel where 3 p.m. Sunday services in French continue the tradition begun in 1575 (see page 22) you see the Romanesque shell of the quire of the 1100s which survived the fire of 1174. Below St Gabriel's Chapel excavation revealed fragmented floors of a Roman temple with votive offerings. The **Son of Man** statue of Christ by David McFall, completed as he was dying, was originally designed for the Christ Church Gate but makes its own moving impression from ground level as McFall insisted, once Ringwald's figure occupied the gate niche in 1992.

The open space now largely car park was the lay cemetery lying beyond the Norman gate to the monks' cemetery. This gate has now been moved to be the entrance to the War Memorial Gardens beyond. To its left is the big fifteenth-century house called Meister Omers after an earlier priory lay administrator. Now a King's School boarding house, it was the grand Canterbury staging post of Cardinal Beaufort, bishop of Winchester. Rounding the Corona you find the ruins of **the twelfth-century Infirmary** with its pillars scorched by the fire of 1174, and its infirmary choir of the 1160s. The Choir House beside it was the thirteenth-century Table Hall where sick and recently bled monks could eat meat and a richer diet.

It shared its cook with the prior who in the later Middle Ages had a grand new lodging in the Green Court nearby. The building and tower in flint to the south side of the present Deanery is the visible vestige of this period when the prior had a separate household of twenty-two servants. At the Reformation it became the **Deanery** being deemed 'the only place fit for the reception of important persons', but was partly burnt out in 1569. There was plenty of stone from the monastic ruins and leftover bricks from Bell Harry so the restorers gave the building its present brick front. During the Second World War it was the home of Dr Hewlett Johnson, 'the Red Dean', and was damaged in the air raid of June 1942. Nevertheless the dean gave a home to the bombed-out vicar of St George's and other homeless victims of the Baedeker raid. On our arrival in 1955 we were startled by the huge banner stretching across the Deanery façade 'Christians Ban Nuclear Weapons' which faced King's scholars of whom Hewlett Johnson was chairman of the governors. When training as a city guide I was shown the dormer window and its ledge where Gandhi would meditate during his 1930s visit to the Deanery at the height of his civil disobedience campaign in India. However controversial in the world, many in Canterbury loved the dean not least for his encouragement of the Canterbury Festivals which produced T.S. Eliot's *Murder in the Cathedral* and Dorothy Sayers' *Zeal of Thy House*. Hewlett Johnson wanted a modern contribution to the cathedral's treasures and a thank-offering for its escape from destruction during in the war. Glass in the south-east transept had been destroyed so Ervin Bossanyi, a Hungarian refugee, was commissioned to create four new stained-glass windows. In 1956, the year of the Hungarian uprising in Budapest, the Peace Window was inserted, in which Christ embraces children of all races. The Salvation Window (see colour plate 3) followed in 1958, in which the imprisoned soul is released by an angel. Above are two smaller windows showing Christ walking on the water and St Christopher, the patron of all travellers. Their brilliant colours are in dramatic contrast to the splendid thirteenth-century Miracle Windows and a fitting memorial of the troubled twentieth century.

We now encounter the three great priors, Wibert the engineer, Henry of Eastry the autocrat and Thomas Chillenden the businessman, who created most of the monastic buildings between

The Deanery. Gandhi's dormer window and the brick frontage of the Deanery occupy the site of the monks' bath house, part of Wibert's water engineering.

1140 and 1411. Busy archbishops were the titular abbots of Christ Church so the priors on the spot strove to enhance their status with spectacular works, financed by skilful management of the priory estates. Lands covering eight counties but concentrated in Kent were made to yield maximum profit as each responded to market conditions of their day and streamlined their administration.

In the 1150s Wibert built the **Infirmary Chapel** and the beautiful **Romanesque Treasury** with its iron-barred windows where he centralized and filed his accounts. His masterpiece, the Water Tower, stands nearby in the Infirmary cloister. Spring water was piped over two miles through five settling tanks and the city wall to this building whence it flowed to all parts of the enclosure. Complemented by an ingenious sewage system it would for centuries keep monks, their visitors and successors healthier than their neighbours.

Water Tower Garden. In addition to the text description you can see the roof of the Chapter House and a glimpse of St Andrew's Tower with its conical top.

Wibert's Hall and Gate. The surviving half of Wibert's guest hall with its Norman staircase is part of the King's School; its War Memorial and Victorian School House are visible. Wibert's gate was adapted and heightened by Chillenden.

There is no better place to appreciate the patchwork blend of periods when you stand facing the **Water Tower** of 1160, topped by Chillenden 250 years later so that monks could wash en route to midnight and dawn services from Lanfranc's 1080s dormitory on the right. The blitz-damaged Cathedral Library rebuilt in 1953 occupies only half the dormitory while a modern herbarium occupies the remaining undercroft. The brick late seventeenth-century library stands on the thirteenth-century pillars of Henry of Eastry's Prior's Chapel while the tower of his Cheker building tops the 1960s Wolfson Library. The fifteenth-century Bell Harry Tower crowns it all. Wibert's St Andrew's and St Anselm's towers on the eastern transepts were part-financed by loans from Canterbury's Jews with whom his relations were excellent; they even rented their synagogue from the priory (now Abode Hotel).

A brief summary of the King's School's long history appears on page 45. Wibert's Great Gate, adorned among sundry fantastic beasts with King David and a mermaid, and his adjoining new guest hall are now part of the School in the Green or domestic court of the monastery. The famous **Norman staircase,** designed to bear the weight of the last cistern of his water system, has thereby been able to survive the centuries. Henry of Eastry after 1285 built the brewhouse in the Green Court which, with the adjoining bakehouse and fodder store have been adapted by the school. Their day-pupils' house, Michinson's, occupies the site outside Wibert's Gate where the school in Christopher Marlowe's day occupied Eastry's old almonry; archaeologists found marbles and clay pipes hidden under its floor.

When elected prior, Henry of Eastry at forty-six was deemed 'a safe pair of hands' who would not last long. His predecessor, Thomas Ringmer, had left in disgrace on the discovery of a blatant forgery of Becket's 'will' in favour of the monks; as a deranged hermit he received a small pension from Eastry. The only prior's tomb remaining in the cathedral is that of this abrupt and masterful man who lasted a further forty-six years dying at ninety-one while celebrating mass. By competitive tendering, farm specialisation and short leases he cleared debts amounting to two years' revenue, doubling priory income. He still spent huge sums on the stone quire screens and gates, the Chapter House with its fine arcaded seating, the cloisters and the Cheker building from which a chosen few administered the entire finances.

We have met Chillenden financing the nave. Its construction involved **rebuilding the cloister** south walk where you can see the novice school's seats and traces of where partitions created study carrels. He persuaded Archbishop Courteney to finance this 'road to Martyrdom' ending at the murder site; the other three walks needed another solution. John of Sheppey's figure on a blue background (see colour plate 4) adorns the vault outside the Chapter House. This patron of all fund-raisers is said to have written over 200 begging letters to the mighty of fifteenth-century Europe which have created the matchless array of heraldic shields on the vaults, designed to be reminders for the monks' prayers; they include those of the Eastern and Holy Roman emperors. Keen eyes may spot two modern additions. The royal visit of 1946 is commemorated by the arms of George VI, his wife and two daughters appearing in the north walk; the Pope's visit in 1982 is marked by his arms with Archbishop Runcie's and Prince Charles' above the western entrance to the cloister (see colour plate 5). Stephen Lote the architect added his master Yevele's grey-ringletted head near the Martyrdom Door, where the springing of his vaulting mars the splendour of the thirteenth-century door which still shows its original colouring.

Chillenden added tops to Wibert's Gate and water tower and gave Eastry's **Chapter House** its magnificent Irish-oak roof and east window. Here monks heard a daily chapter of St Benedict's 'Rule' and dealt with domestic and disciplinary problems. Numbers had shrunk from the Norman 130 to about forty-five by 1411 but by switching from hands-on farming to a leasing policy Chillenden had increased revenue eightfold. Swamped by pilgrims he created the surviving wooden Pentise and Chillenden Chambers, now the Archdeacon's House and formerly occupied by Edward Hasted, Kent's eighteenth-century historian. Chillenden finally went out into the town to build a vast multi-purpose inn, the 'Cheker of the Hope' (see page 87).

Leaving the cloisters, the **Archbishop's Palace** lies on the right. Lanfranc's original building of 1070, in which Becket and the knights had their last argument in 1170, lay across the present driveway at right angles to the west end of the cathedral. The undercroft of Becket's solar was found in excavation when Mrs Runcie designed a garden outside her dining room which occupies the end of Lanfranc's annexe for his clerks, in turn incorporated into Elizabethan Archbishop Parker's Palace. When a new palace was built in the 1890s for Archbishop Frederick Temple and his successors this wing became part of what you glimpse today through the gates. Lanfranc's old hall had been superseded long since by the huge new hall, second only in size to Westminster Hall, built by Hubert Walter and Stephen Langton in the early 1200s. A magnificent building, used to entertain Elizabeth I, it was demolished on Parliamentary orders after 1643 along with much else in the Archbishop's Precinct. Some fragments remain in the King's School's Walpole House. The remaining buildings were then let out as houses, yards and workshops.

Above: Henry Yevele. A tribute from his pupil to Edward III's great architect whose work you see in the nave and at the Westgate.

Right: The Chapter House. This building's two phases by Eastry and Chillenden were obscured by tiered seating during the Civil War when it became 'The Sermon House' where most services were held. The Victorian glass in the east window tells Canterbury's story from St Augustine to Queen Victoria.

The Buttermarket. The favoured side of the White Bull pilgrim inn is seen behind the war memorial, a favourite spot with tourists and buskers. Starbuck's and Debenham's crypt restaurant were parts of other pilgrim inns.

This story of how each generation in turn raised the funds to build, to maintain and to beautify this unique building may prompt you before leaving to add your contribution in this century to the current cathedral appeal. For instance, a single walling stone costs £60.

Leaving through the **Christ Church Gate** under a vast Tudor rose you see the final work, a tribute to Tudor peace and the marriage of Prince Arthur to Katharine of Aragon. Outside, the arms of Henry VII, the Welsh dragon, Lancaster whippet and Beaufort portcullis are flanked by those of the bridal pair and Tudor nobility (see colour plate 6); finished in 1517, the arms of Wolsey and the last two priors appear. The visit of 1521 by the then Queen Katharine and her husband Henry VIII, dead Arthur's brother, accompanied by her nephew the Emperor Charles V would have seemed a bitter irony to watchers in 1538. Twenty-six cartloads of gold, silver and jewels from Becket's demolished shrine, trundled off to the Tower of London. The King replaced the monks with a Dean and Chapter of Canons by 1542 by which time three more wives had followed Queen Katharine to the grave, the scaffold or divorce.

The frieze of angels bearing shields depicting the Passion story flank a niche from which jubilant puritans in 1643 hauled Christ's bullet-scarred statue. The wooden doors were replaced at the Restoration by Archbishop Juxon, while the gate itself was restored as the first work of the Cathedral Friends in the 1930s. Klaus Ringwald's figure of Christ of 1992 now surveys today's tourist throng from the niche, somewhat lugubriously in my view.

The Buttermarket

The Buttermarket, so called for the last 400 years, has been here since the 1100s, when it was called the Bullstake. Butchers would provide juicier Sunday joints by baiting a tethered bull to death with dogs. The ringside apartments on this side of the fourteenth-century 'White Bull' pilgrim inn cost more to rent than those facing Butchery Lane and its sm(see colour plate 5)elly shambles.

When Henry II walked barefoot to his penance in 1174 he ordered that the tolls of this Royal market, amounting to ten silver marks, should be paid forever to Harbledown leper hospital. A cheque for £13.33 is still paid annually to St Nicholas Hospital there, now housing the elderly.

A high cross occupied the site of today's war memorial. Proclamations were read and barefoot penitents were whipped. Mayor Nicholas Faunt, a rich grocer, was executed here for high treason on Edward IV's orders in 1471 for backing a failed Lancastrian attack on London.

A puritan mayor destroyed the cross in 1645, coining farthings from its lead covering, but at the Restoration William Somner, the first historian of Canterbury, and his brother, spent £400 on a market hall. Town and country produce-sellers traded free on the stone pavement below. Upstairs, in one room the city's seven merchant companies met; the other room was let for plays and concerts, the rents supporting the residents of Eastbridge Hospital. A garret above stocked corn to be sold cheap to the poor of suburban parishes if famine struck.

The city rebuilt the Somners' work in 1790 as a roofed market space on sixteen pillars. It was the scene of open voting at elections until 1872. Polling lasted three days and during the heated debate before the Great Reform Act of 1832 riots broke out as Freeman voters from far afield returned to cast their votes even if 'sick, old and even dying'.

The market was replaced in 1893 when Sir Henry Irving unveiled the Marlowe Muse statue here, now outside his theatre. It caused outrage. 'This semi-clad female could be no inspiration of dramatic poetry and insults the cathedral', thundered the local newspaper's correspondent. Laurels were grown round her until she was banished to the Dane John Gardens in 1921 when Earl Haig unveiled the War Memorial which still occupies this space.

two
The Blackfriars Quarter

Standing in the Buttermarket looking down narrow Mercery Lane where pilgrims would have bought their lead souvenir badges of St Thomas or bottles of water supposedly from his well, it is hard to visualise eighteenth-century coaches manoeuvring their way down this Lane. They had to continue down equally narrow **Sun Street** past the Sun Inn where Dickens used to stay. Only in 1803 was the new relief road, now Guildhall Street, cut through from High Street to Palace Street and thence to Margate. The Sun Inn, itself a fifteenth-century building, was the Elizabethan home of John Lyly, author of *Euphues* and a fellow-pupil of Christopher Marlowe at the King's School. The street had led to the Rush Market; the red pump above the corner shop of Palace Street/Orange Street remained in use until piped water was installed in 1867.

The Blackfriars Precinct

From 1236 this low-lying area between the branches of the Stour was colonised by the Dominican or preaching friars, whose land was held for them by trustees. Their precinct extended from Orange Street to the north-western city walls. They had preached to Archbishop Stephen Langton and set up their eleventh English house here where about thirty black friars established their base and ran a hostel for visiting preachers and academics en route for London and the universities. A guest hall was therefore built on the other side of the river; it has been lovingly restored by private owners as a much-used youth and community centre under its fourteenth-century roof. It can be seen from the Friars Bridge.

Canterbury Theatres

Orange Street was the site of Sarah Baker's Theatre in Georgian times. This illiterate child of circus performers was a redoubtable business woman who ran a winter season here and at two other Kentish theatres. Its façade is clearly identifiable at 'Merchant Chandlers'. When it closed, the local artist Sidney Cooper built the Theatre Royal in 1861 at his own expense and to his own design in Guildhall Street where it flourished until 1926; it is now part of Debenhams. The present Marlowe Theatre in the Friars which draws large modern East Kent audiences is a converted cinema of 1933 due for further expansion. The despised and neglected Marlowe Muse Statue was moved here to be unveiled again by Sir Ian McKellen for Marlowe's 4th centenary in 1993.

St Peter's Street

On the corner of the Friars and St Peter's Street a depiction of the old Black Friars Gate, demolished in 1787, surmounts the corner shop. It fell victim to Alderman James Simmons

Right: The Sun Inn. The original windows and brick nogging were exposed during recent restoration revealing the city's wealth made from the pilgrim trade. Charles Dickens would stay here while gaining local colour for *David Copperfield*.

Below: Blackfriars. The timber roof of the Guest Hall on the left bank was donated by Henry III; the reader's pulpit projects from the refectory opposite. Friars listened silently at dinner to a fasting brother while he read improving texts.

The Marlowe Theatre and *Kitty*. August 1933 saw a race between two 'super cinemas' to open first. Each went up in a mere sixteen weeks and seated 1,500 and 1,700 fans in novel luxury. The Friars Cinema became the Marlowe; the Regal survives today as the Odeon.

and the Georgian improvers who widened the street and enforced the cutting back of timber-framed houses and all 'pediments, porticoes, projections, posts and rails whatever'. You can see in St Peter's Street how the owners enjoyed modernizing their houses with sash windows and false-brick 'mathematical tiles' hung on the exposed laths and mortared in.

The Methodist Church

The handsome Methodist Chapel of 1811 was a huge achievement for its poor congregation who had outgrown Wesley's original octagonal 'pepper-pot' on the site of the Friends' Meeting House in the Friars; he had favoured octagonal chapels distinctively different from Anglican churches. In his latter years Wesley had been an annual visitor to this regimental town. Fifteen hundred oak piles had to be sunk into the marshy ground of their new site to support the new church.

Dr Rigden of the Canterbury Dispensary deplored the poor health of denizens in St Peter's parish, with their pulmonary and rheumatic complaints. Their expectation of life in the 1840s was twenty-four for women and twenty-nine for men; at the top end of the town St George's parish boasted figures of thirty-four and thirty-nine.

St Peter's Church itself lies back on the Roman street alignment. It is plain that the bottom part of the tower is of late Anglo-Saxon build; the two western bays inside are early Norman. Viewed from the Marlowe Theatre its three gables show its evolution from one narrow nave to a thirteenth-century aisle and then a large fifteenth-century extension to cater for the survivors of defunct parishes following the Black Death.

Thomas Sidney Cooper

One who survived this unhealthy area was Thomas Sidney Cooper born in 1803 in the cottage now part of Canterbury Christ Church University Art Department. His father went off with his regiment leaving mother to rear five children on dressmaking. At the age of nine the Archbishop gave him £5 for a cathedral sketch; at twelve he started work painting coach panels, then scenery at Mrs Baker's Theatre. At seventeen, already producing lithographs, he won a studentship at the Royal Academy which he could not afford to accept. Finally at thirty his first RA painting won him fame and fortune. His rural paintings of sheep and cows would appear at the academy in unbroken succession from 1833 to 1902 (still a record) when Edward VII bought two for his grandchildren's nursery at Sandringham. From his return to Canterbury in 1850 until his death at ninety-nine he was a generous benefactor to many city bodies. He founded his College of Art as a memorial to his mother at her cottage and yard, 'to encourage young talent and provide the facilities I had been denied in youth'. He designed its surviving Ionic portico and taught there into his eighties, charging 1d a week to students of whom Mary Tourtel of *Rupert Bear* fame was one. The Royal Museum has many of his paintings and lithographs including *The Monarch of the Meadows* - a large bull to rival Landseer's *Monarch of the Glen*.

Monarch of the Meadow. Victorian nouveaux-riches loved rural scenes. It was rumoured that by agreement Landseer painted dogs and deer; Cooper stuck to sheep and farm animals. This bull, Charlie, belonged to a friend. (Canterbury Royal Museum & Art Gallery Copyright reserved 2007 ©)

Palace Street: Saints and Sinners

Palace Street was created by Archbishop Lanfranc in the 1070s when he made his three-acre palace enclosure, evicting twenty-six Saxon families. This diverted the Roman street running from Worthgate by the castle which only reappears round the corner in the Borough and Northgate. Lanfranc, that Norman new broom, had begun to weed out the calendar of Saxon saints. It took a determined campaign by two monks Osbern and Eadmer to salvage the reputations of St Alphege and St Dunstan, their two great Saxon patrons.

St Alphege Church was under archbishops' patronage from 1086 and is documented before 1200. Hauled from a hermitage by St Dunstan whose successor as Archbishop he became, Alphege restored church life after the ninth-century Viking invasions. When in 1011 Thorkell the Tall and Olaf the Stout returned to demand the cathedral treasures Alphege, greatly loved and trusted, led Canterbury's resistance. After a twenty-one day siege the cathedral was fired, the people killed or enslaved and Alphege taken to Greenwich a prisoner (see colour plate 9). There at a drunken Yule feast he was pelted with ox bones and finally killed by his repentant guard who said 'We would not treat our horses so'. The Christian Dane, King Canute, restored the

The Mayflower. Robert Cushman had submitted to the church court on his release from Westgate prison to be eligible to marry his wife at St Alphege Church opposite.

body of our first martyred archbishop to the cathedral in 1023. The church, made redundant in 1982, became home to an environmental and urban studies centre. It was a valued community resource for study, exhibitions, meetings and refreshment for twenty-five years but has recently had to close. The King's School hopes to use it for drama studies and it will continue to host the thriving Festival Club in October.

Further down Palace Street is the sixteenth-century frontage of **Conquest House** (see colour plate 10), an antique shop. Like so many of the city's twelfth-century houses it once had a front courtyard, later built over. Inside the shop some of the original stone walls of Gilbert the Citizen's house survive. Here, early in the afternoon of Tuesday 29 December 1170, Becket's murderers, FitzUrse, de Tracy, Le Bret and de Moreville, arrived after a well-liquoured lunch with Becket's enemy the Abbot of St Augustine's. Entering the Archbishop's Precinct opposite, they left their armour under a mulberry tree to burst in on the servants' dinner after Becket had left the dais. This early hall lay adjacent to the cathedral's west end. An hour's furious argument ended with FitzUrse cracking his fingers and renouncing his allegiance before the four stormed out to rearm. Becket was bundled by his entourage through a cellar passage to the cloisters while the knights forced entry to the barred hall with tools left by some repair men. For what happened next see page 24. After the murder they looted the palace and made off eventually to Knaresborough Castle, held for Henry II by de Moreville. Sent by the Pope on penance to the Holy Land, they are all thought to have died there within a few years.

The American Connexion

Many Americans stop to admire a painting of the *Mayflower* above a Palace Street café. To this inn a Canterbury grocer, Robert Cushman, returned in 1620. He had formerly been imprisoned for puritan fly-posting 'during the hours of divine worship' and afterwards migrated to Leyden. Commissioned by other puritan exiles there to find a ship to hire for the perilous journey to New England and religious freedom, he negotiated the *Mayflower* deal here. He wrote back, 'We have took a good liking to one about 180 tons for a greater we cannot get, but a fine ship it is'. But for the unseaworthiness of the ill-named *Speedwell,* which had to be left behind, he would have captained this sister ship on the 1620 voyage. Another Canterburian, the tailor James Chilton, sailed on the *Mayflower* and was a signatory of the famous Mayflower Compact. He was soon followed by two members of our refugee Walloon community; Hester Mayhieu, ancestress of Winston Churchill, and Philippe de la Noye, ancestor of Franklin Roosevelt. Cushman himself took out a relief ship in 1621 but returned to London where he died in 1625 still fund-raising for the colony.

The Strangers

This part of town was the first home of 100 families welcomed in 1575 as 'a poor and patient people' who would run their own church, school and social care from the cathedral crypt given them by Queen Elizabeth I. They had fled Roman Catholic persecution in the Low Countries, had overcrowded Sandwich and, as the council hoped, would fill empty properties, introduce new weaving skills and never burden the parish poor rates. By the 1600s this industrious group was employing 2,000 local workers on their 'New Draperies'. Like all immigrants who keep to their own ways they attracted ill-feeling in hard times. During bread riots in the 1630s a placard read 'Living five and six families to a household they get a living when the Englishman cannot'. Palace Street shows their traces in the row of weaving loft windows inserted in a double-jettied house in Turnagain Lane and very clearly in the shop opposite the King's School entrance. Here are the gratings of cellars where wool was stored, the shop where goods were sold, the

rows of high windows lighting the two weaving floors and the garret below the gable where the workers slept. Yet it is also the very handsome house of Avery Sabine, from a successful immigrant family, who became a councillor and thrice mayor during the Civil War, and was imprisoned in Leeds Castle in 1648 while mediating with the puritan forces besieging the city. The pargetting decoration and the earliest version of a Red Indian carved into the corner post display his wealth. The famous crooked door was the result of Victorian tampering with the central chimney stack which has now been stabilized.

King Street

The Blackfriars Refectory
Lying off King Street behind Palace Street are the remains of the Blackfriars. After preaching against Henry VIII's divorce the prior had prudently taken the next boat to France, leaving his brethren to be dissolved in 1538 by the apostate Richard Ingworth, Bishop of Dover who had once been head of the English Province of the Order. Alderman Bathurst's weaving factory which had been established in the church within the year would later become the Strangers' Hall. The refectory was where all the cloth was examined, stamped and certified before sale. They began with fine woollens known as the 'new draperies', particularly black bombazine in great demand for the many funerals of the day. Celia Fiennes in the 1690s described their latest silk

Opposite left: Turnagain Lane. On first arrival the Walloon weavers, like those living here, used St Alphege Church before they were granted the Cathedral crypt. When later they began to marry local girls many of their names appear in this church's records.

Opposite right: Avery Sabine's house. This reconstruction of the house in its first glory reveals its multiple uses; you will probably prefer to photograph its crooked door.

Right: A Red Indian. Following the Virginia settlement after 1608 and the visit of Pocohontas printed images of native Americans became popular. This carved dragon post is possibly one of the first everyday sculpted depictions.

fabrics – 'alamodes, lute strings, paduasoys, damasks and watered tabbies'. When a second wave of Huguenot refugees had arrived from France in the 1680s, many immigrant families moved to Spitalfields as brocade designers. Others sent one enterprising family member to London, retaining a small firm in Canterbury. After 1681 the Weavers Company of London recorded many old Canterbury names, for example two Mankey boys apprenticed to James Leman. He and his partner Peter Lekeux, a captain in the militia, were the first two Huguenots to join the Court of the London Weavers' Company. By 1706 seventy-two Canterbury families were recorded in the silk industry of both cities. Those remaining in Canterbury began to 'marry out' to Freemen's daughters and were then able to carry on different trades and become Freemen themselves with a vote. Silk weaving began its long slow decline from 1,000 looms in 1676 to just one by 1830 (see page 66). By Daniel Defoe's day in the 1720s the Refectory had become a Baptist chapel where he preached. He described Canterbury as 'a general ruin, a little recovered'. Meanwhile another successful immigrant had made a home in the domestic buildings of the friary. Dr John Peters MD was baptized a Roman Catholic in Armentières, married by Calvinist rites in Lille and was buried in St Alphege Church as an Anglican 'of the manor of Blackfriars'. His descendant conducts Walloon and Huguenot walks during the Canterbury Festival and names like Lepine, Terry and Fedarb are found in the telephone book. The Blackfriars Refectory is now the King's School Arts Centre.

The Synagogue. The women's baths lie to the right. The pillars reminiscent of the temple of Karnak were part of an Egyptian vogue dating back to 1802 after the Rosetta stone had reached the British Museum.

The Jews

Behind Avery Sabine's house lies a reminder of another immigrant community. Cromwell readmitted the Jews to England in 1654 and by 1760 a sizeable Jewish community acquired a burial ground in St Dunstan's parish and built a synagogue. The Jewish cemetery off Whitstable Road has been restored with a lottery grant and contains 150 graves dating from 1760 to 1930. The synagogue survived until the South-Eastern Railway Co. in 1846 created the present level crossing over St Dunstan's Street and the building was demolished. The Jews were surprised and delighted to receive generous subscriptions for the rebuilding from non-Jews.

They chose the vacant site of the long-dissolved Knights Templar in King Street, next to the dissolved Chantry of the Black Prince as symbolic of the toleration of their contemporary British neighbours, so unlike the era of the Crusades. They built in Egyptian style as is easy to see, Gothic reminding them too forcibly of medieval persecution. The corner stone was laid in the presence of the mayor, aldermen and magistrates of Canterbury as well as of the Chief Rabbi and Sir Moses Montefiore.

By 1931, when only three practising Jewish families remained, the synagogue was closed and sold. It is now beautifully restored, with features like the women's gallery and ritual baths intact, as a concert room for the King's School. It is occasionally used by today's Jewish community recently augmented by our two universities.

Beyond the synagogue lies St Radigund's Street, named for the hostel which St Radigund's Priory at Folkestone once maintained here.

The Mill. These durable cast iron remnants are a sad reminder of a big concern. Simmons built barns, stables and a shop opposite and rebuilt the bridge after the city wall there had been demolished.

Roman city wall. This section of the Roman city wall was only revealed when cottages were demolished to continue the city ring road towards the Westgate. This plan would have left the Westgate marooned on a traffic island and was abandoned.

The Mill

In 1792 the energetic entrepreneur and street improver, Alderman James Simmons (see page 67), commissioned John Smeaton to rebuild the old Abbot's Mill of St Augustine's. A weather-boarded 100ft monster rose to dominate the skyline. Powered by only two wheels with a 5ft 3in fall of water, six working floors produced 500 quarters of flour a week. The mill was an important factor in attracting three regiments to Canterbury during the Napoleonic Wars, increasing its population by 2000 and boosting job opportunities. The mill burnt down in 1934; the Millers' Arms pub contains interesting pictures before and during the fire. Its garden contains the remains of the millrace.

Simmons also improved the public bathhouse where 'citizens of either sex could enjoy cold bathing in privacy and convenience'. The site is now the Dolphin pub; the pool was situated in the garden.

The Roman City Wall

From the small public garden behind 72 Northgate you can see the wall of St Mary Northgate Church. It incorporates nearly 30ft of original Roman wall created between AD 270 and 290 at a time when the Saxon Shore forts at Richborough, Reculver and Dover were being refortified against German invasion. Sharp eyes can detect the line of Roman crenellations just below the small blocked Norman window which sits on one of them. Below the roof line you can detect the brick uprights of the fifteenth-century crenellations when the wall was heightened to deter the French. Viewed from the side it is clear that the later work was thinner and scrappier than the Roman original. The rest of the city wall in this quarter was demolished in 1769 and the stone used to widen the King's Bridge in the middle of the High Street. The fine Kentish hall-house, now Radigund's Restaurant, therefore lay inside the walls.

St Mary Northgate

The church had begun life as a chapel above Roman Northgate and is recorded in Saxon documents. As this poor suburb expanded with incomers, immigrants, widows and workers in dirty trades the church too expanded backwards. The gate itself survived the battering of Margate coaches until it was demolished in 1830. The continuing church then received its unattractive Victorian frontage; it, too, is now used by the King's School.

The King's School

The school's colonisation of Blackfriars, the Synagogue, St Alphege and St Mary Northgate has been mentioned; you meet its beginnings on the opposite side of the Borough at the blocked-up and modern Mint Yard Gates. A brief period as an Archbishop's Mint gave this yard its name.

The school's claim to be the oldest in England rests on the seventh-century Christian mission's need to educate its converts. Early documents frequently refer to schools around the Precincts, but an archbishop's school certainly existed in the Almonry in 1259, sited outside Wibert's Great Gate to the priory (see page 29). Its own set of priests supervised the school and distributed charity, such as the 3,400 loaves given out annually in memory of Archbishop Lanfranc.

The school's life can be reconstructed from documents. The master was paid one-third of £1 a year; boys were admitted at the age of ten if they could read and sing and acted as 'fags' to sick monks. Royal and priory bursaries supported several poor boys and deficits in the annual accounts were made up by the priory. After 1371 some boys even went on to Canterbury College at Oxford, now just one quadrangle of Christ Church.

When in 1542 Henry VIII established the New Foundation of a dean and twelve canons to run the cathedral after the priory had been dissolved, Archbishop Cranmer fought hard for a Canterbury university. He wanted five additional professors and a student body of 120; he had to settle for a King's school of a master and usher on £20 and £10 a year and fifty poor scholars. Cranmer wrote 'Poor men's children are many times endued with more singular gifts of nature than the gentleman's son'. After two temporary homes the school settled in 1573 in the converted Almonry which had been given to the Chapter by the last Roman Catholic archbishop, Cardinal Pole.

When Victorian boarding houses and other buildings were added in the period after 1853 the new Mint Yard Gate was created. Today the school occupies most of the buildings surrounding the Green Court (see page 30). Under Canon Shirley, whose dynamic headmastership from 1935 started today's rapid expansion, the large Assembly Hall of 1957 was even built in the medieval Archbishops' Precinct. The school is now fully co-educational and now occupies the Royal Palace and later Missionary College at St Augustine's (see page 120).

From Thomas Linacre, Henry VIII's doctor and founder of the Royal College of Physicians, to Michael Foals, first Briton in space, there is a long roll call of famous Old Boys. Among early ones are Christopher Marlowe, in whose days boys could only play games on the Green Court speaking Latin or Greek, and William Harvey, who truanted to study the slow blood circulation of frogs on Sturry marshes. Hugh Walpole and Somerset Maugham bequeathed their libraries to

St John's Hospital. Norman privies. Behind each end of Lanfranc's dormitory were twin toilet blocks, continuously used from 1085 to 1948. Well ventilated and flushed by rainwater from the roof, they drained towards the river beneath the orchard, now a car park.

their old school; even Montgomery of Alamein spent a term here. He was one of generations of soldiers, bishops and administrators whom the school has sent out from a place described by Walter Pater as 'where one seems diminished to nothing at all amid the grand waves, wave upon wave, of patiently wrought stone'.

Two Ancient Almshouses

St John's Hospital

Continuing along Northgate past more weaving lofts at the Canterbury Institute of Heraldic and Genealogical Studies you reach our oldest charity. In his late seventies Archbishop Lanfranc in 1084 founded two institutions which, over 900 years later, still cater for the elderly. St Nicholas' Hospital at Harbledown was originally for lepers but St John's Hospital was for thirty men and thirty women, tended by canons from over the road where he founded St Gregory's Priory. Part of his Norman dormitory, portions of his cut-down church and one toilet block, in use from 1085 to 1948, survive among today's Victorian flint cottages and a new extra-care block opened in 2000.

After the Reformation when, under Mary Tudor, ten sisters were expelled for holding Protestant opinions, archbishops regulated the continuing almshouses. From this period date

Above: St John's Hospital today. Visits are possible by prior arrangement to view part of the original Lanfranc dormitory of 1085 and its latrines, the continuing church and the post-Reformation refectory seen here in the converted end of the dormitory.

Right: Sir John Boys. Sir John was from the new breed of professionals founding almshouses named after themselves rather than saints. Inmates honoured them in life, no longer praying for their souls after death.

Penny Theatre. After many years as an ironmonger's, the theatre once again hosts popular musical evenings and drinks at today's prices.

the kitchen with refectory above, made out of the left-hand end of Lanfranc's dormitory, the gatehouse and the half-timbered frontage on Northgate. The chapel font is a reminder that pensioned old widowers proved attractive to Northgate's many poor women. Stern orders from the 1680s onwards banished wives and children from the enclosure and enforced residence on the men. Lands sold to the University of Kent in 1964 financed a modernisation programme which rents from Northgate properties still enhance.

Jesus Hospital

St Gregory's Priory held the Archbishops' archives and after the Dissolution of 1536 the prior's lodging became the home of lawyer-archivist Sir John Boys, whose monument is in the cathedral nave. Surveying his poor neighbours from his grand residence he founded Jesus Hospital in 1595, also still existing further along Sturry Road. As well as chapel and lodging it incorporated an apprentice school so that poor youths would not grow up to 'idleness and stealing but become apt members of the commonwealth'. Sir John's endowments have since 1881 been attached to Simon Langton Grammar Schools so still serve education.

On the site of the Priory Canterbury Christ Church University have named their student hostel Lanfranc.

Military Road

Northgate, this poor suburb, gained new life during the Revolutionary and Napoleonic Wars. Cavalry, Artillery and Infantry regiments were attracted to Canterbury for its strategic position, modern turnpiked roads and ample corn and fodder supplies and brought with them population, jobs and prosperity. Barracks were erected along the line of old Prior Wibert's twelfth-century water pipes. They used the water supply and troops could exercise on Scotland Hills where the springs rose. Military Road, now part of the ring road, soon attracted a Roman Catholic primary school, still flourishing there, which catered for soldiers' families. Close-packed houses for them were built across the erstwhile gardens of Sir John Boys' house in old St Gregory's Priory. A new Anglican St Gregory's Church was built off Military Road; it is now a concert hall for Christ Church University.

The soldiers' houses which had become overcrowded slums were replaced by post-war council housing; the barracks area is now a large housing estate and the site of the city council's offices. Old residents remember when doctors and police visited in pairs and red uniforms fluttered outside Northgate's many pawnshops before pay day. A surviving vestige of those days is the **Penny Theatre music hall** near St John's Hospital. Victorian Canterbury was notorious for over 100 pubs, the consequence of 6,000 acres of hop gardens, thirteen small breweries and plenty of thirsty soldiers.

The officers' presence also supported Victorian social life with theatrical performances, band concerts, cricket matches and charitable functions. Some of their Regency houses remain in St Dunstan's Terrace with mews and cottages for their servants in New Street behind. The cathedral is full of regimental monuments and the Buffs regimental chapel in the south-west transept is the scene of a short daily service at 11 a.m. The East Kent Regiment, raised under Elizabeth I, were called 'The Buffs' after their Canterbury leather coats; their regimental museum is housed in the Beaney Institute. Amalgamated regiments still occupy by turns the modern barracks at the top of St Martin's Hill and a bandsman blows the ancient Burghmote Horn at each annual Mayor-making.

THE BLACKFRIARS QUARTER AND OUTSIDE THE WESTERN WALLS

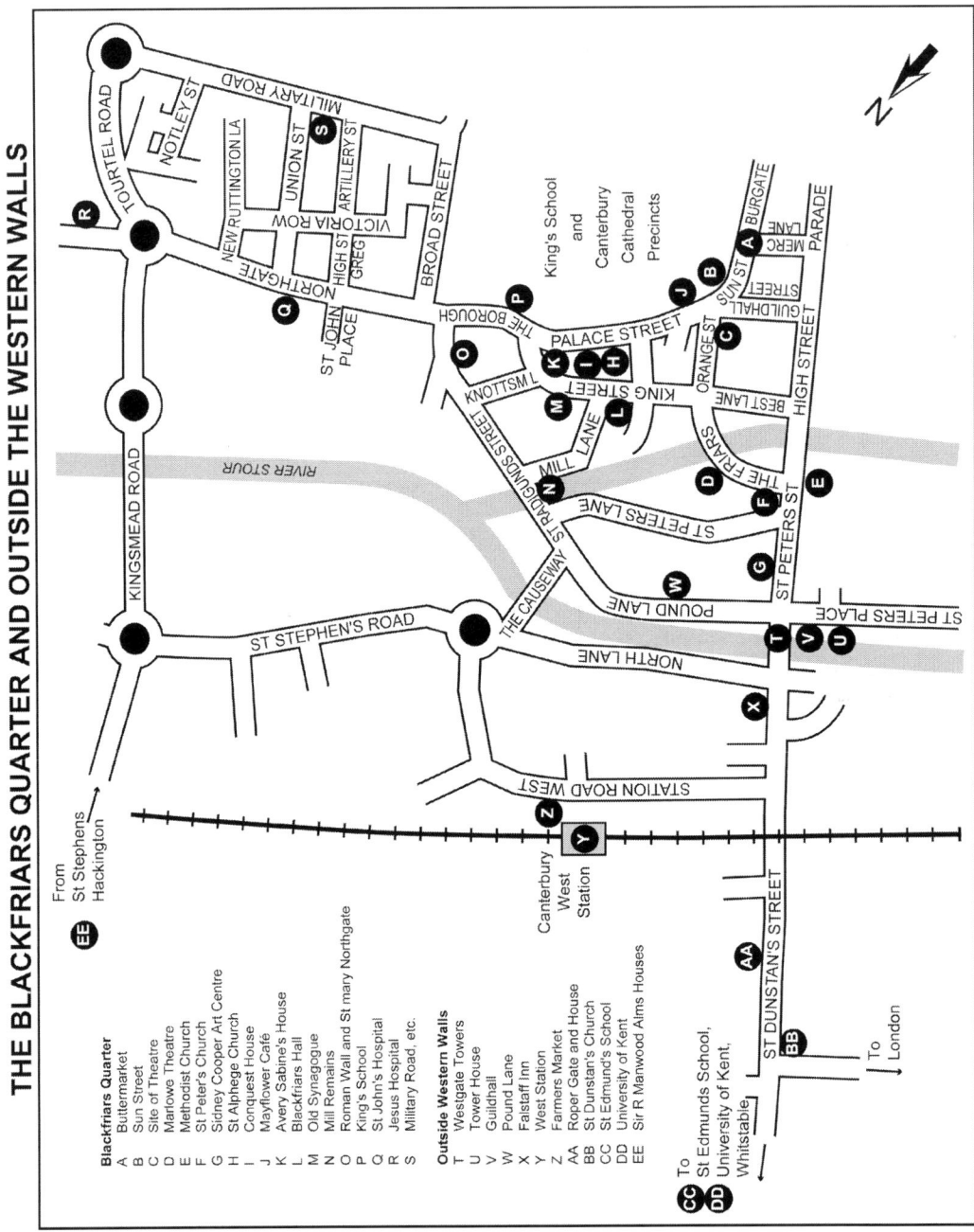

Blackfriars Quarter
A Buttermarket
B Sun Street
C Site of Theatre
D Marlowe Theatre
E Methodist Church
F St Peter's Church
G Sidney Cooper Art Centre
H St Alphege Church
I Conquest House
J Mayflower Café
K Avery Sabine's House
L Blackfriars Hall
M Old Synagogue
N Mill Remains
O Roman Wall and St mary Northgate
P King's School
Q St John's Hospital
R Jesus Hospital
S Military Road, etc.

Outside Western Walls
T Westgate Towers
U Tower House
V Guildhall
W Pound Lane
X Falstaff Inn
Y West Station
Z Farmers Market
AA Roper Gate and House
BB St Dunstan's Church
CC St Edmund's School
DD University of Kent
EE Sir R Manwood Alms Houses

CC To St Edmunds School,
DD University of Kent, Whitstable
BB To London
EE From St Stephens Hackington

three
Outside The Western Walls

The Westgate

Across the river where Westgate stands lay the other half of the first-century Iron Age settlement. For two more centuries it became the Romans' industrial suburb full of blacksmiths and tile and pottery kilns. The London Gate taking Watling Street towards London lay southwards where a stone marks its site in the Westgate gardens. There the fifth-century silversmith buried his hoard (see page 7).

When the Roman walls went up from AD 270-290 a new gate was needed when they decided to exclude this suburb and use the river as an addition to the defences. By late Saxon times the guard-chamber above it had become the Church of the Holy Cross, served by a guild of priests.

Archbishop Simon Sudbury financed the rebuilding of Westgate in 1380 as his part in strengthening defences against the French. He employed the King's master mason, Henry Yevele (see page 31), who designed the new gate while working at the castle. It was the latest thing in its day with keyhole gun-loops on the three floors of its drum towers. Machicolations for pouring unwelcome liquids on attackers can be seen and holes where chains drew up the drawbridge – no longer there to deter lorries and buses from squeezing through.

It was unfinished in 1381 when the Peasants' Revolt erupted against Sudbury's hated Poll Tax, for he was also Chancellor. The gate proved no deterrent to Wat Tyler's rebels who burst in to taunt the monks, loot Sudbury's Palace and capture the castle in order to burn the county's legal and financial records. After their suppression the gate was finished but in much rougher fashion, as the top floor and parapet reveal, since Sudbury had been murdered by the rebels in London and cash had run out.

Westgate became the city gaol where John Howard, the eighteenth-century prison reformer, found seven men chained on straw. Condemned prisoners had to walk the length of the High Street, ropes round their necks, to the gallows on Oaten Hill by the Dover Road. St John Stone, the Whitefriar who defied Henry VIII in 1538, was dragged from here on a hurdle to a traitor's death on Dane John Mound. The eighteenth-century street improvers still needed the prison so Westgate alone survived the demolition of all the other gates between 1787 and 1830. Only the Mayor's casting vote saved it in 1824 when a wagon loaded with hop-bags got stuck; but an Edwardian mayor even 'improved' it by adding gun loops pointing in on the city in the interests of symmetry. The battering the gate receives from today's traffic still provokes argument. A door under the arch leads up spiral stairs to the **Westgate Museum,** housed in the old cells. This part of the city museum service also provides a magnificent view of the whole city from the roof.

The Medieval Walls
Originally the city paid for the restoration of the walls from Westgate anti-clockwise round to Burgate, while the Cathedral Priory paid for everything in a clockwise direction. Geoffrey

Westgate. This view reveals the gun loops, machicolations and the hole taking a drawbridge chain. Compare the meticulous stone-laying at the bottom with the rougher finish at the top.

Tower House. The Victorian flint house blends well with the original tower, the walls of which are twice as thick. In Pound Lane nearby you can compare this adaptation with two more towers converted into cottages.

Chaucer as Clerk of the King's Works had the duty of inspecting the result since the city had received murage grants from the King. Perhaps this visit gave Chaucer the idea for a set of stories since the *Canterbury Tales* was probably written in 1387 soon after the walls' restoration. The stretch from the Westgate to the castle was further demolished on Fairfax's orders after the suppression of the second Civil War in 1649 which had been sparked off by Christmas Day riots here. Large parts of the priory's work came down in 1769 in the St Radigund's area to provide stone to widen King's Bridge in the city centre. All that remains to see today is Sudbury Tower and its neighbouring tower in Pound Lane to the north and **Tower House** in the Westgate Gardens. This became the home of the first lady to become mayor. Mrs Catherine Williamson whose husband owned the tannery was in office in 1939-1940 and wrote a book *Though the Streets Burn* about wartime Canterbury. The Williamsons gave both house and gardens to Canterbury after the war. The house is now the Lord Mayor's Parlour for civic entertainment and the public gardens are beautifully maintained. Other standing stone fragments are the

The Guildhall. The fourteenth-century church has been sensitively adapted for its new function as the modern Guildhall of the district council.

picturesque imports of the Williamson family. The rebuilding of Westgate involved the rebuilding of **Holy Cross** Church beside it, one of only two entirely fourteenth-century churches in Kent. When it became redundant it was turned into the city Guildhall after the lamented demolition of the war-damaged medieval Guildhall in the High Street.

City Government

Canterbury had a Portreeve from AD 780, replaced by two bailiffs in late Saxon times when the city's six wards were created. The Burghmote Horn which summoned Aldermen to meetings is still sounded at every annual Mayor-making. Our charter, granted by Henry VI in 1448, made Canterbury 'independent of Kent forever', a state which lasted until 1974. Today's city council also administers Whitstable, Herne Bay and the surrounding area and has retained the right to a Lord Mayor.

Pound Lane, opposite the Guildhall, is named after the medieval enclosure for stray animals. The Victorian gaol, which replaced the prison in the Westgate, housed until recently pupils of the Kent Music School who were taught in the converted prison cells. The Pound Lane car park lies over a short-lived attempt to make Canterbury a spa town. In the 1690s a chalybeate spring was found at 6ft and a sulphurous one at 4ft, each yielding a barrel an hour. Unfortunately the waters of both became cloudy in the air and could not be bottled, unlike Tunbridge water. When Celia Fiennes visited the wells, set among gravel walks and exotic plants, she drank half a glass to music accompaniment and pronounced it nauseous and possibly numbing. Yet it was advertised as 'sovereign for diseases of the breast, consumption of the lungs, most stomach disorders, rheumatic gouty pain, scurvy, melancholy distempers, vapours, stoppages, scab and itch – and agrees best with old, weak and decayed constitutions'. The spa craze passed and no parked car has yet subsided into the springs.

The City Arms. Henry II's royal leopard struts above one place where Becket's symbols were not erased – the three Cornish choughs or beckets. The silver crown was presented by King Cnut when he returned St Alphege's body. 'Ave Mater Anglia' (Hail Mother of England) is a Victorian motto.

The Falstaff. As the White Hart this was one of the six coaching inns supplying weekly coaches which transported travellers to London for under £1. Through tickets allowed passengers to reach Paris by Channel packet for 3 guineas.

St Dunstan's Street. Recent excavations at 'Fusion', in the foreground, found evidence of Roman and Saxon occupation. An astrolabic quadrant used in navigation, surveying and time-keeping was a very rare discovery. It dates from the 1380s, Chaucer's day; he wrote a book on astrolabes for his son.

St Dunstan's Street

Since the Westgate shut at curfew, late pilgrims would spur their horses to a 'Canterbury pace' or 'canter' to achieve a safe lodging. If they failed they had to stay in the St Dunstan's suburb outside where a number of inns catered for them.

Inns

The **Falstaff**, originally called The White Hart, is a good example with vestiges of its original courtyard and the Tap in North Lane for ostlers and servants when it was a regular stage-coach station. Other fine timber-framed houses and inns remain, dating from the fifteenth to eighteenth centuries, such as the Hospice Shop and Fusion. This latter was where Charles Dickens imagined Agnes Whitfield living in *David Copperfield*. The sixteenth-century Unicorn pub was not the only one acting occasionally in its history as a bawdy house; the Café des Amis Mexican restaurant on the corner of Westgate Grove had a rear exit for soldiers avoiding the military police. The street has remained full of inns and restaurants to this day, partly caused by the coming of the railway.

The railway

The Canterbury-Whitstable, 'crab and winkle' line, was a world first, opening in May 1830 five months ahead of the Liverpool-Manchester Railway. It issued the first season tickets and combined train/boat tickets, but suffered the fate of pioneers. The Stephensons' *Invicta* locomotive could not have coped with the hill on which the university now stands and only ran along a flat section to the coast; the carriages had to be hauled on cables by stationary steam engines up to and through a tunnel under the hill. This is now filled with concrete since a university building above threatened to subside into it. The cost of repairs to the locomotive and improvements to Whitstable Harbour among other miscalculations led to bankruptcy in 1841. However, a public cycle track now follows the line and *Invicta* is displayed in the Museum of Canterbury. The South-Eastern Railway Co. took over the line in 1844, built the handsome West Station and created the level crossing in St Dunstan's Street which demolished the synagogue (see page 41). The original 'Goods Shed' of the old railway remained in use and is now, suitably named, a flourishing farmers' market and restaurant.

West Station. Trains ran to Whitstable until 1954 although the small tunnel, made for carriages only, remained a problem for larger locomotives. The excellent brown-field housing development opposite occupies the site of the original station yard.

Roper Gate. By 1550 brick techniques were highly developed. Specially moulded bricks were hand-finished, and the crow-stepped gable incorporates vitrified bricks and raised diaper patterns.

Roper Chapel. The bones in the vault below this memorial were too disturbed to confirm that the skull is definitely Sir Thomas More's.

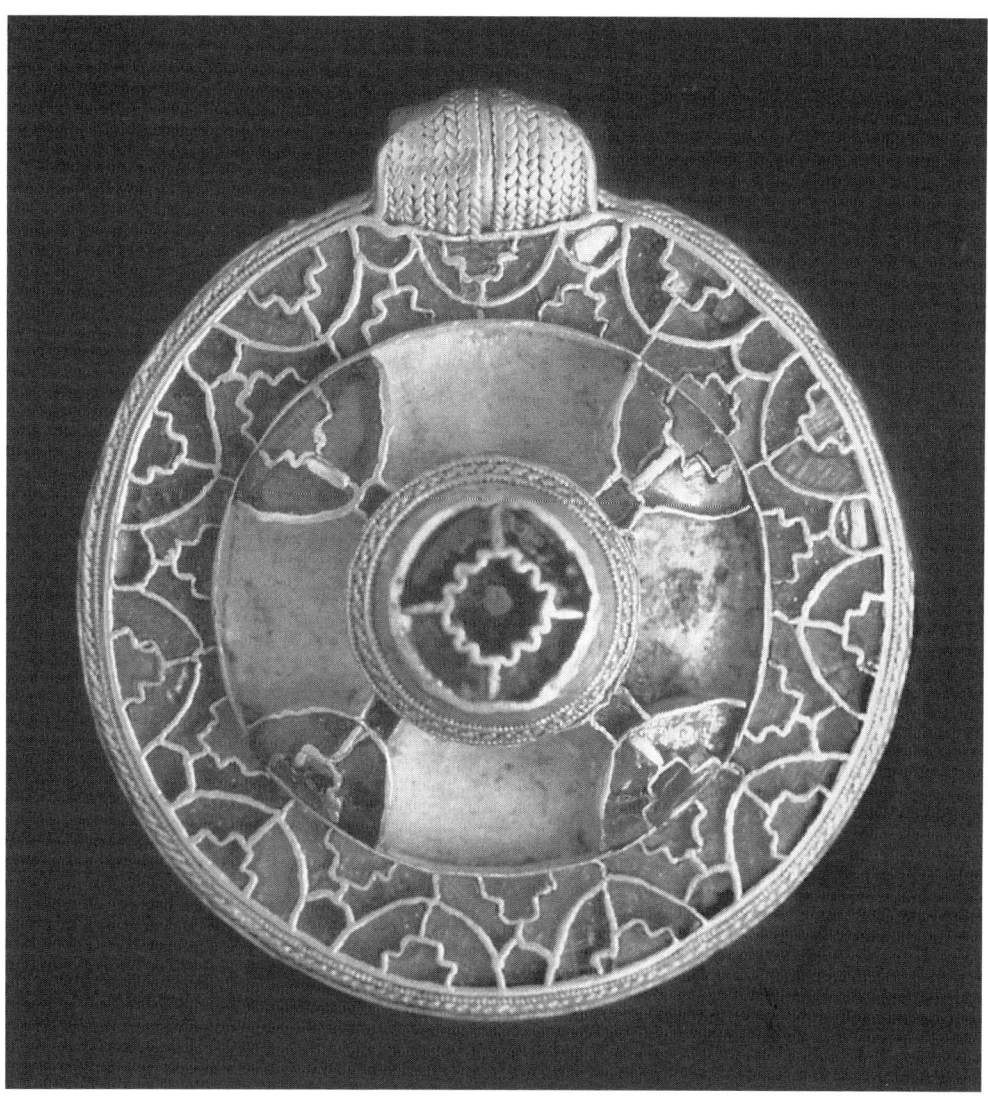

Saxon bracteate. This find overlay a corner of the Roman cemetery on the site of sheltered housing at Cranmer House.

The Ropers

A handsome Tudor brick gateway near St Dunstan's Church is the sole survivor of the Ropers' home. It became a brewery in 1787, a later owner building Roper House, now a residential home for the deaf. This successful legal family added a brick chantry chapel in the fifteenth century to the south-east corner of their parish church. In time John Roper lodged in Sir Thomas More's London home during his legal training and married his favourite daughter Margaret. While Chancellor, More was a frequent visitor to Canterbury. When Henry VIII executed him for denying the Act of Supremacy, Margaret begged for his head exposed on London Bridge. A skull in the crypt of the Roper Chapel is thought to be his; an annual service, attended also by Roman Catholic pilgrims, is held in the chapel, now largely his memorial.

St Edmund's School. This snowy scene accentuates the neo-Gothic chapel (1855) so important to its Anglican founders. The neighbouring school, Methodist Kent College (1885), originally had to walk the boys to their city church. Both these flourishing schools are now co-educational.

St Dunstan's Church

Outside, herringbone stones in the north wall and north-west corner stones reveal the pre-Conquest origins of St Dunstan's Church, tended by the same guild of Saxon priests who ministered to Holy Cross and St Mary Northgate. Like some other Canterbury churches it was founded on a large Roman cemetery; in 1982 the latest of many artefacts was excavated nearby. Our first Christian jewel of about AD 600 is displayed in the Museum of Canterbury. A pendant in gold and filigree, resembling Kentish pagan work like the Kingston brooch, bears a central cross once inlaid with mother-of-pearl.

Among the bells rung each week is No. 5, cast in 1325 by William le Beletyre; the youngest two bells date from 1775. The church had a collection of fifty-one plays which were performed outside the inns of St Dunstan's Street in the pilgrim season; the 'Sacrifice of Isaac' was the most popular. A market cross stood outside the church where a haberdashery fair was held.

In 1174 to start his spectacular public penance for his suspected involvement in St Thomas

The University of Kent. Rutherford College, with its picture window framing the Cathedral, the Senate House and the Templeman Library, named for the first vice-chancellor, are all elements of Holford's original design.

Becket's murder, Henry II left his horse here. Changed into sackcloth he then walked barefoot to the cathedral for his scourging by every monk and all the church dignitaries.

Origins

On the corner outside St Dunstan's Church, you are standing on Canterbury's origins. Prehistoric trackways ran along the high ground each side of the wide Stour estuary. Here, London and Forty Acres Roads follow this route; St Martin's Church stands by the corresponding track on the opposite bank.

Following Caesar's attack on Bigbury hill fort in 55 BC, the Iron Age Belgae seem to have deserted it five years later for a settlement which they called 'Durovernon', the strong place in the alder grove. This was the lowest point at which the Stour could be forded and St Dunstan's Street is the road which led to the ford and round it a western settlement grew. Beyond today's Westgate the larger fortified township developed in the St Margaret's Street area. This would become the heart of the Roman tribal capital Durovernum of the Cantiaci.

Were you to continue northwards towards Whitstable, up St Thomas' Hill through successive ribbon developments of the nineteenth and twentieth centuries, you would reach Philip Hardwick's imposing **St Edmund's School** of 1855 in Victorian Decorated style. Its high hall and chapel in Kentish ragstone crown the hill. Built for the Clergy Orphan Foundation of 1749, it is now a thriving co-educational school from ages four to eighteen, particularly strong in music and drama. It also educates the cathedral choristers who board in the Precincts at the Table Hall (see page 26).

Further along this cold and miry scarp lie the 300 acres of the **University of Kent**, one of the six new universities founded soon after 1958. All sought enough space on the edge of a historic town and Kent's site, with spectacular views of the cathedral, encouraged Lord Holford to design

Manwood Almshouses. There is no chapel since the church is a few yards away, or a hall since Sir Roger gave the residents Sunday dinner at his manor house and two loaves a week collected from a shelf by his tomb after service.

the first two colleges, Eliot and Rutherford, to maximise the impact of this view. Financial curbs and students' preference for the campus village now developed at Park Woods ended the project of a collegiate university of eight colleges. Only Keynes and Darwin Colleges were added in very different styles, which do not convey a harmonious impression. All four have now added extensions in the architectural fashions of their dates.

The university opened to students in 1965 and is now a great success with over 15,000 students and a budget topping £100 million. In 2000 it entered into partnership with the University of Greenwich and other bodies to open their Medway campus, expanded at Tonbridge and in 2004 launched a joint initiative with four French universities, the 'Reseau Universitaire Transmanche'. About 11 percent of the university's intake comes from beyond the European Union. It also provides space for a Korean-style building, incongruously named Chaucer College, where Japanese students spend one or two years, mainly in English and business studies, before completing their degrees in Japan.

The founders hoped that the university would expand downhill to share facilities with the city; although this did not happen the Gulbenkian Theatre, a cinema and a series of open lectures are much frequented. The impact on the cultural and economic life of a sleepy cathedral city has been dramatic, not least because many of the teachers have served over the years on the city council. A town of under 50,000 has difficulty in sharing its housing stock with two burgeoning universities especially in these days of 'buy-to-let' investment.

In September 2007 the university's first woman vice-chancellor took office. She is Professor Julia Goodfellow, a distinguished biochemist.

Returning from the University of Kent by St Stephen's Hill you reach the picturesque suburban village once Hackington. **St Stephen's Church** contains some features from Archbishop Baldwin's proposed college of canons here which so alarmed the Christ Church monks that they bombarded the papal court with letters of objection. An exasperated Richard the Lionheart whisked the Archbishop off to his Crusade, there to die at the siege of Acre in 1190. The church was finished and a manor house built near the Green in 1227 by Simon Langton, brother of the Magna Carta archbishop.

Elizabeth I gave the manor to a wily lawyer MP **Sir Roger Manwood** who founded the continuing row of almshouses in 1570. The parish clerk tended them from the end house, now the Old Beverlie Inn where Kentish 'bat and trap' is played. Sir Roger's grand tomb by Colt, the creator also of the Queen's tomb, dominates his chapel in the church. He died applying for the post of Lord Chief Justice while under house arrest on embezzlement charges, but has left us his almshouses and his grammar school in Sandwich.

The **Roman Catholic Hales family** (see page 118) acquired the estate under Charles II and a century later built a new Hales Place on what is now the Terrace approached by Hales Drive, an avenue planted at that time. The last heiress, Miss Mary Hales, born in France and convent-educated, inherited 4,000 acres and ran the estate from 1856 despite being a Carmelite nun dispensed from vows of poverty and obedience. She failed to establish first a nunnery then a Benedictine priory in the extended building and, when bankrupted in 1879, sold to the Jesuits. They ran a school for 260 French boys for the age of ten and then a seminary until 1923 adding yet more extensions. In a derelict state the buildings were finally bought and demolished by a contractor for its three and a half million bricks, its stone, timber and fittings, partly used to create private housing on 'garden city' lines in the 1930s. A large post-war housing estate followed in the midst of which is preserved the tiny Jesuit chapel and graveyard to which Miss Hales' body was moved in 1928; she had died in poverty at the age of forty-nine.

four
Greyfriars or The South-West Quarter

By the time in the 1200s when the friars arrived, Further most English cities found them sites in suburban areas where the poor lived and worked at dirty trades. In Canterbury the soggy area between the two branches of the Stour were undeveloped and undesirable. While the Blackfriars colonised the north-west side of the main street the Greyfriars spread on the south-west side but both within the city walls. Before looking southwards it will be convenient to describe buildings each side of the main street from the Friars (see page 36) up to Stour Street.

No. **53 St Peter's Street,** now Zizzi's Restaurant, hides the oldest secular building in Canterbury with a long history behind its Victorian brick front. The flint and stone wall of Luke the Moneyer's stone house of 1200 with its pointed doorway form the back wall of the front restaurant, itself converted from the shop with its Elizabethan plaster ceiling built over the original courtyard. An amazing aisled hall with scissor-braced roof lies behind, all that remains of William Cokyn's short-lived almshouse of 1203 which was soon united with its neighbour, the Eastbridge Hospital. In 1529 John Thomas who made the points attaching doublets to hose built on a kitchen and ordered the lovely hall panelling carved with grapes and the tools of his trade (see colour plate 13) John Cogan, the lay administrator of the archbishop's estates under the Commonwealth, finding he was descended from Cokyn, founded his own almshouse here for six poor clergy widows in 1657. When the estates reverted to the Church in 1660 the widows were rescued by Canon Aucher and remained there until Victorian Gothic villas, since sold, were built for them in London Road. It is worth eating here to appreciate all these ghosts.

Passing All Saints' Lane with its row of fifteenth-century cottages you reach a stone plaque which records the widening of the King's Bridge by 10ft in 1759 with stone from the city walls. This twelfth-century bridge still carried heavy traffic until the street was pedestrianised in the 1980s. **The Weavers,** three medieval houses with twentieth-century 'antique' timbering, on its west bank is but the most celebrated of many weaving establishments in the riverside parishes using water for fulling and dying. Until comparatively recently one loom still demonstrated the 'Canterbury muslins' with which the declining trade tried for a while to vie with intermittent Indian imports during the French wars when French silks were unobtainable and high-waisted Jane Austen dresses were in vogue. A linen warp and silk weft produced the fabric devised by James Calloway, a master silk weaver. Once stiff French silk returned after the wars and crinolines came in, Canterbury weaving was in terminal decline and poor weavers filled up the workhouse every winter. James Calloway however was an exact contemporary of James Simmons who features at the next building, King's Mill. They were colleagues as Freemen and Improvement Commissioners; Calloway's public spirit initiated in 1769 the 'Friendly Society for the Cultivation of Useful Knowledge'. His library and museum were eventually housed in a Grecian style building in Guildhall Street. Bought by the council in 1846, they became the nucleus of today's collections in the Beaney Institute (see page 90).

On the opposite bank stood **King's Mill**, recorded in Domesday Book, given by Henry II to Rohesia, Becket's sister, during his visit in penance in 1174. A public lavatory or 'forrens' was attached to the mill wall opposite the Weavers; a ducking stool in such an unsavoury spot would add to the punishment for nagging wives. The replacement is modern, for by 1799 the mill had long been corporation property and was leased to Alderman **James Simmons** who would not tolerate such things. This successful businessman was already operating the huge new Abbot's Mill downstream. Since King's Mill impeded the flow to his new waterwheels Simmons persuaded the council to let him demolish the mill to build his own handsome house there (now ASK restaurant). Timber-framed, it is clad in mathematical tiles to look like brick. A blue plaque records the city's debt to an amazing man. Native-born and King's School-educated he returned from training as a stationer in London in 1768 to found our continuing local paper the *Kentish Gazette*. With a partner he founded the Canterbury Bank (now Lloyd's) further up the High Street. As alderman and mayor he not only drove through street improvements (see page 36) but pulled down all city gates save the Westgate Prison and half-financed the new Guildhall Street. This was to ease the flow of stage and mail coaches on which Canterbury's economy depended. Principal among his many benefactions was the rescue of a rubbish area by the city wall to create Dane John Gardens, which he gave to his city, now a prize-winning civic amenity (see page 113). His monument crowns the mound which once bore the keep of the first Norman castle. He died as MP in 1807, still hoping to promote a Canterbury canal to the sea.

All Saints' Lane. Phipson's water colour of 1887 is recognisable today. Such scenes horrified Ruskin who described Canterbury as 'vulgar, moral and narrow to the uttermost – such an air of ale, tobacco and sanded floors'.

The Weavers. The immigrant tradition continues; the Italian restaurants occupying the buildings today call themselves 'Little Italy'.

Next door stood **All Saint's Church**, a victim of his improvements. The original medieval church is outlined in the pavement round Whittards. Its porch and tower were lopped off and a Regency replacement church was later built further back in Best Lane. After this church's demolition in the 1930s it became a small open space.

On the opposite side from Simmons' house lies **Eastbridge Hospital**, founded by Edward FitzOdbold in 1190 for poor pilgrims. Its first Master was Becket's nephew, Ralph. It can be visited to see the undercroft where the wayfarers slept on straw and which, in post-reformation times, became the old men's dormitory. Upstairs is the refectory where the neighbouring Greyfriars brought the evening meal. A magnificent thirteenth-century fresco of Christ in Majesty (see colour plate 11) surrounded by symbols of the evangelists adorns the north wall, a permanent reminder of the Last Judgement for the pilgrim diners. When two Elizabethan archbishops rescued the foundation from greedy courtiers who had sold off beds and fittings, Archbishop Parker added the extension to the west end and two bays were lost from this hall to create apartments for old women. The hall was used as an apprentice school run until 1861 by the Master of the continuing almshouse. Christopher Marlowe, the dramatist, probably started his education here, beginning and ending the day with prayers in the chapel. This restored treasure has a wonderful timber roof part of which supported a cupola. By selling some endowed lands to the university in the 1960s all accommodation has been modernized and a number of Anglican Franciscans once again visit today's residents. Glancing at the unbroken list of masters, the deaths

Eastbridge Hospital crypt. When restored in the 1930s half a metre of compacted dirty rushes were removed to reach the pillar bases. A wash place existed to the right, projecting over the river.

of three between 1349 and 1351 are a solemn reminder of how diseased pilgrims brought the Black Death to Canterbury, killing nearly half the population.

From the Eastbridge Hospital for 150yds up this side of the street was the twelfth-century frontage of **the city's Jewry**. From 1160 to 1290 when Edward I expelled the Jews from England our first asylum seekers enjoyed cordial relations with their Christian neighbours. Hannah the widow is recorded selling an inherited property to a Christian priest next door. The cathedral monks, building continuously, needed loans and were happy to lease and even sell properties to Jews who alone were allowed to lend money at interest. Even their synagogue on the site of Abode Hotel was owned by the Cathedral Priory. Canterbury was second to London in having eight mints; the Royal Exchange (opposite at French Connection) controlled quality and next door was Jacob the Jew's stone house (recorded in the pavement). He had financed the synagogue and paid over half of the £235 which Canterbury's Jews contributed to Richard the Lionheart's ransom. His Jewish coiners worked in Whitehorse Lane, then called The Mint, which runs back to a street still called Jewry Lane. In the good years 400 Jews packed this area, some arriving from Stamford and York where their treatment was worse. However, under

Jewry Lane/Jew's Stone House. These and the Old Synagogue are the only vestiges of our first immigrant community.

Henry III they were loaded with fourfold extra taxes and in 1278 all the Jews were imprisoned in the castle where graffiti from the Psalms survived until 1780. Six were hanged for coin-clipping and by the year of the expulsion most had fled abroad. In 1640 the historian Somner recorded inside the hotel 'a stone parlour mounted upon a vault, ascended by many steps, a good part of what was our Canterbury synagogue'. (for the later Jews see page 42). No trace survives today and nor any of the Roman forum on which 'Abode' stands.

The Greyfriars (Franciscans)

In September 1224 nine patched and barefoot followers of St Francis of Assisi, four of them native-born, landed at Dover to found an English mission to the poor, to the sick and at the universities. Narrowly escaping hanging as undesirable immigrants, the cathedral priory sheltered them for two days before Alexander of Gloucester gave them a room at his new hospital for poor old priests in Stour Street. They would huddle round the embers of the central fire at evening sharing one mug of gruel. Four of them went on to London and Oxford so that when, in 1267, John Digge, a former city bailiff, bought the Canterbury group a permanent home on Binnewith island forty-nine other English friaries were flourishing. This marshy area behind Poor Priests' Hospital became the Franciscan Precinct, eventually stretching westwards to cover eighteen acres. Intermittent excavations since 1919, most recently by *Time Team* in 2000, have found vestiges of the large preaching church with its characteristic 'walking place' between nave and chancel. The gate on St Peter's Street is now reduced to a door leading to an overgrown right of way beside the shop 'Third Eye'. A seventeenth-century house beside today's public

Greyfriars. After the Lovelaces, this building was used by the Presbyterians who eventually joined the Congregationalists. Today's descendant is the United Reformed Church in Watling Street.

The Museum of Canterbury. Eight centuries of occupants might marvel at today's popular additions featuring Rupert Bear, Bagpuss and the Clangers, the creations of Canterburians Mary Tourtel and Peter Firmin.

access to the site and old bridge replaced the Stour Street Gate. Here you find a pleasant riverside garden and the remaining **thirteenth-century friary building**, now a restored chapel where a small group of Anglican Franciscans hold services; they also visit nearby Eastbridge Hospital as their predecessors did. The building, perhaps once a mill, probably became the guest hall with the warden's lodging above. The thirteenth-century friary contained about sixty friars, reduced after the Black Death to the thirties. It had a good library and under the famous Franciscan Archbishop John Pecham (1279-1292) the friars instructed the cathedral monks and preached throughout the diocese. As one of the six English Observant friaries under royal patronage they remained popular to the end. Unfortunately, two of them with two cathedral monks supported the visionary nun Elizabeth Barton who was attacking Henry VIII's divorce in 1533-34. They suffered the full horror of a traitor's death at Tyburn and the remainder stayed under house arrest until the friary was dissolved in 1538. Snapped up for £100 by an official of the court handling monastic property, Greyfriars was then bought by the grandfather of Richard Lovelace the cavalier poet. Could the ghosts of the imprisoned Greyfriars have influenced his poem 'Stone walls do not a prison make/ Nor iron bars a cage'?

The Eastbridge Hospital now owns the site of the building and the city has created public paths and a garden.

Poor Priests' Hospital (Museum of Canterbury)

Following the cathedral fire of 1174, the monks paid the minter Lambin Frese to move his dangerous furnaces from Burgate to this riverside site in Stour Street. Part of Frese's stone house, fireplace and doorway were found during excavations in 1981-82. In 1220 his son sold the site to Alexander of Gloucester who built his hall and kitchen for poor priests at right angles to the house with the active encouragement of Archdeacon Simon Langton. His endowments, well-managed, paid for the fourteenth-century rebuild which is what you mainly see today. The fine perpendicular windows of the master's lodging and chapel and the new kitchen beyond the remodeled screens passage are of this period. A series of open hearths found in excavation lie below a trap door but, looking up, smoke-blackened roof timbers testify to centuries of open fires.

When Queen Elizabeth was given the ruinous foundation on her fortieth birthday in 1574, she promptly returned it to the city to become its 'House of Correction'. This is when an upper floor with new windows and fireplaces was inserted. It continued as workhouse, 'harlots' harbour' and charity Bluecoat school into the nineteenth century when first a new workhouse and then the Simon Langton Grammar Schools incorporating the old endowments made it obsolete. Police station, organ builders, regimental museum and health centre succeeded on the site until its splendid conversion as the Museum of Canterbury. Here, imaginatively displayed, are all the important archaeological finds and historic legacies including Roman cavalry swords, the Christian pendant of AD 600, Becket memorabilia and the *Invicta* steam locomotive.

The replacement of bombed cottages by the building of **Temple Mews and Mulberry Court** revealed interesting Roman finds. In the early 400s, a mystery burial within the temple precinct broke funerary taboos. Long thought to be a family of parents, two children and an old pet dog, new analysis suggests that they were not buried but thrown into a disused pit, may not be related and were possibly left exposed for a time, despite the jewellery adorning the females. Mulberry Court is built over the wooden piling, drains and roadway of Roman Watling Street as it crossed this marshy area to follow roughly the line of the A2 to London and part of the A5 to Chester.

Maynard and Cotton Hospital

Founded in the 1180s by one of the wealthiest moneyers 'Maynier le Riche', for three men and four women living round a central chapel, this continuing almshouse served a poor quarter of the city. In 1604 Leonard Cotton, ex-mayor and wealthy pewterer, added three more dwellings, stipulating that the mayor should nominate occupants from the two neighbouring parishes. The early records, sent to London for a legal case, perished in the Great Fire of 1666 but the hospital remained a city concern. When the old buildings collapsed in a storm in 1703 the city promoted the rebuilding in today's form as a row of cottages with a Flemish gable round the chapel. Admission became non-denominational and, as an alderman was always Master, Alderman Simmons was able in his day to restore its constitution and finances in the 1780s. He is buried in nearby St Mildred's Churchyard. In 1970 two cottages were added to commemorate local miller and mayor, Frank Hooker. The chapel is still used regularly and all the units have been updated to modern standards.

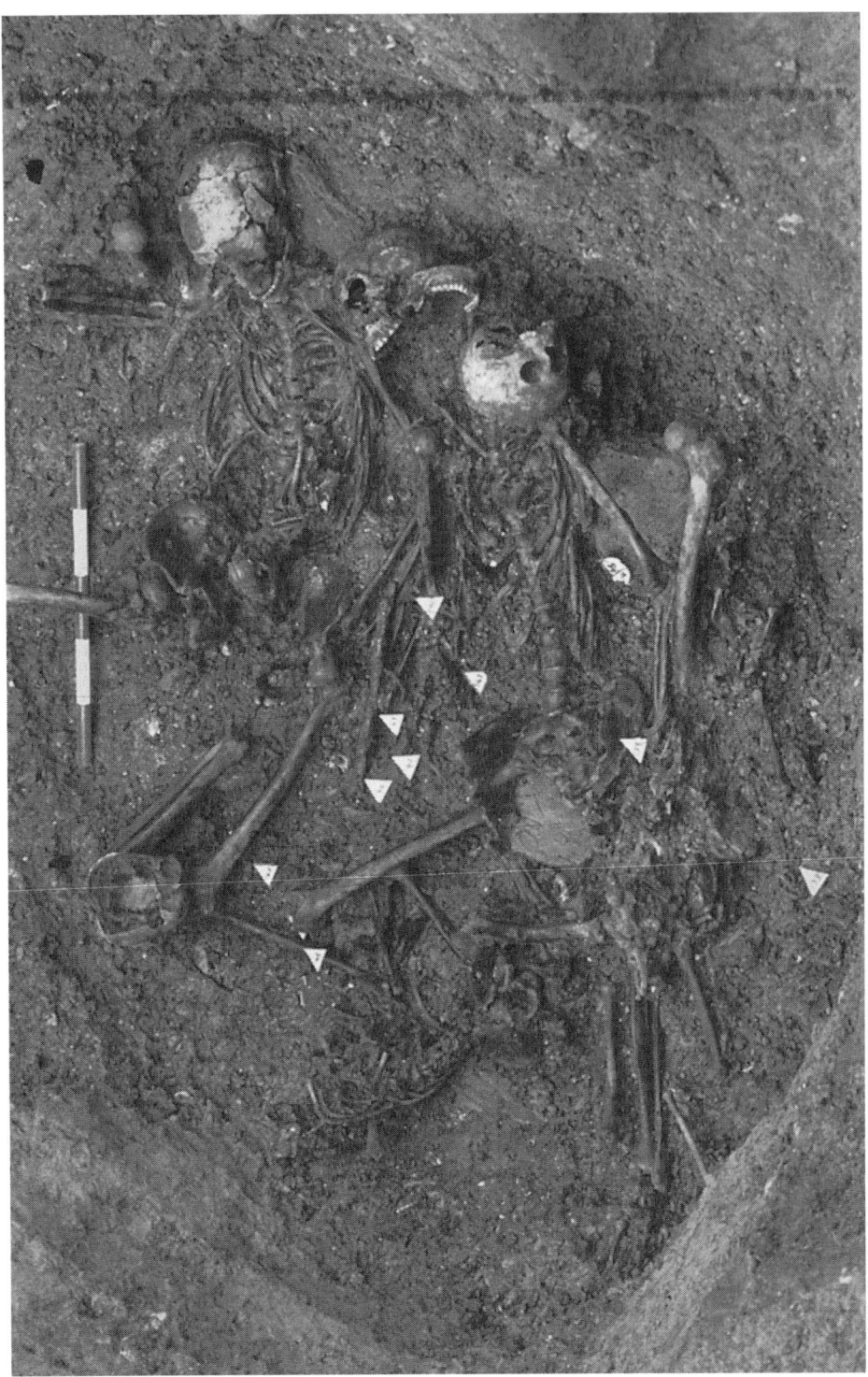

Why were they rich in a declining city? What caused their simultaneous deaths? How did an old dog come to lie on the man's knee?

Maynard and Cotton Hospital. Admiral Rooke, capturer of Gibraltar, was a principal contributor to this rebuild of 1708. His memorial is in the Buffs' Chapel in the Cathedral. This listed building is expensive to maintain to twenty-first century standards

The new housing you see next is erected on the site of a famous tannery for years making leather for Rolls Royce and Jaguar and for the seats of parliament buildings all over the world. The combination of the Stour chalk stream, oak trees and a cattle market attracted the first Williamsons from Fife in the 1780s (see page 53). The site is impregnated with tannery residues making difficult work for archaeologists and developers alike. A possible Roman 'mansio' or staging-post inn is among the few finds of note in an area of pasture inside demolished sections of the city walls.

St Mildred's Church

This is the only Saxon foundation within the walls. It was founded by St Augustine's Abbey after the last Danish siege of 1011. They had acquired from Thanet the seventh-century remains of St Mildred, a royal saint, and had dedicated this church to her in about 1023 when King Cnut gave back St Alphege's body to the cathedral, itself restored. The south and west walls are original and reveal large reused Roman blocks on the south-west corner in typical long-and-short work. After the Black Death the neighbouring parishes, first of St John the Poor and then of St Mary de Castro, were so decimated that remaining congregations went to St Mildred's where fourteenth-century south windows and a new fifteenth-century north aisle were added. The chequerwork of the south chantry chapel is of 1512. Isaak Walton, author of *The Compleat Angler,* who loved fishing for Stour trout, was married here in 1626.

St Mildred's Church. This view shows Anglo-Saxon work on the corner, the fifteenth-century aisle and early Tudor chantry.

Worthgate

Only a plaque indicates the site of this gate, built when the Roman walls went up in the 270s as a single arch set at a dog-leg in the wall. It led to their restored coastal fort at Port Lympne. The Saxons called it 'Wye-gate' (now corrupted) leading from Ethelbert's pagan worship site there. It then became the start of the processional way to the cathedral. The Normans used it as part of their barbican when the castle was built until it was walled up in 1548 when a new road skirted the castle completely. It was taken down in 1791 and adorned a nearby garden before the owner of Lee Priory bought it for his garden hoping that it would 'help maintain the monkish character of the building'. It has now disappeared.

Canterbury Castle

The first Norman motte and bailey castle on the Dane John Mound (see page 113) was soon found to be in the wrong place. A replacement existed by 1089, strategically sited by the Roman gate to Hythe and beside the river. In fact archaeologists have revealed a Roman fort near here at the time of Boudicca's revolt in AD 61.

Henry I ordered the building of the present stone castle between 1100 and 1114. Originally 80ft high, the three-storey building contained royal apartments on the middle floor with chimneys, large windows and a well shaft. These were reached by an external stair. Medieval kings owning

THE WORTHGATE

Worthgate. William Stukely fortunately recorded this gate among other drawings before the eighteenth-century improvers began their demolitions.

much of France needed comfortable staging posts; Rochester and Dover castles provided two more. Besieged by the French in John's reign, it was successively strengthened defensively but was mainly used as the county law court and prison and for the safekeeping of records.

So here the Jewish community awaited execution or expulsion in 1290; here Wat Tyler's rebels in 1381 burst in to seize and burn records of their labour services. Here too under Catholic Queen Mary between 1555 and 1558 forty-one Protestants, including ten women, were held before being burnt alive at Martyrs' Field. Five died of privation in the castle. A letter they managed to throw out reads, 'We, poor prisoners for God's Truth, lie in cold irons and our keeper will not suffer any meat to be brought to comfort us. We write not to the intent that we might not be famished for the Lord Jesus' sake, but they have no law so to famish us and should not do it privily'.

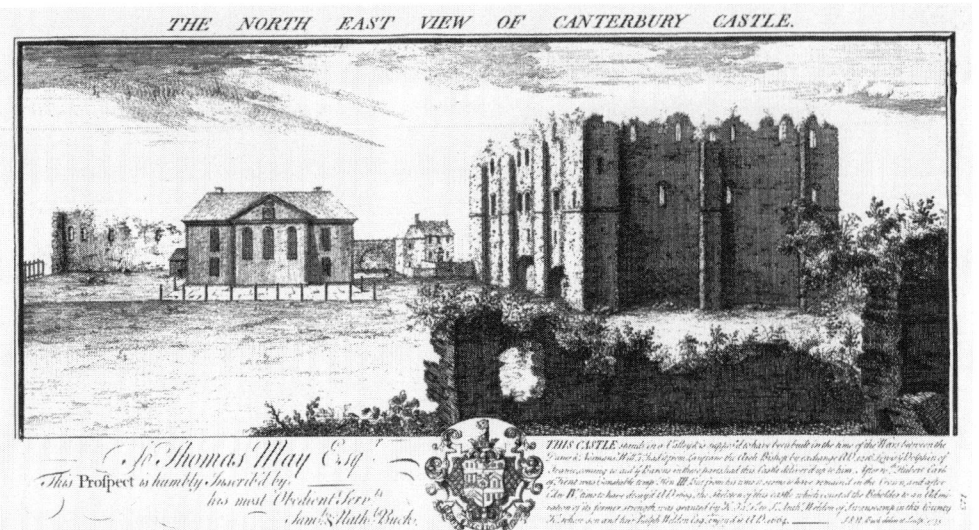

Castle and Sessions House. Since Canterbury's 1448 charter made it independent of Kent, Royal and County jurisdiction was dispensed here. The new County Courthouse and Prison of 1817 were built outside the city limits beyond Longport. (Canterbury Royal Museum & Art Gallery Copyright reserved 2007 ©)

The new County Courthouse of 1730 still stands opposite. It incorporated part of the city wall and was linked by a tunnel to the brick cells below a house adjacent to the castle which survived as the Tudor-style Castle Hotel and was demolished in 1963 for the present roundabout. When both the county court and prison moved to Longport in 1817 a similar tunnel linked the two buildings. The white elephant of a castle, though ruinous, proved immoveable, resisting two attempts at demolition which only destroyed the top storey where the constable and his family had lived. The adjacent new gas works eventually used it as a coal and coke store, to which solution we owe its survival. Barham, in his *Ingoldsby Legend* of the cobbler and the ghost, describes it as 'a well-scooped, mouldy Stilton cheese'. Recent restoration allows today's visitors to understand its layout and varied uses over time.

Before the multi-storey car park next door was built in 1981 a Roman murder mystery was uncovered. Two Roman cavalrymen and their long swords had been crammed into a shallow grave below an inn floor in about AD 300. The swords are displayed in the Museum of Canterbury.

Before continuing along Castle Street towards the city centre you can digress along Worthgate Place, the new road of 1548 skirting the castle, to Wincheap Gate in order to explore that ancient suburb.

Wincheap Gate must have originally resembled other city gates with an upper chamber over the arch. In 1670 a local doctor paid for an entire rebuild, incorporating stone from one of the ruined monasteries; the city council rewarded good Dr Jacob with a civic dinner. The local parishioners petitioned for its eventual demolition in 1770. It bore plaques on each face saying 'Welcome' and 'Farewell'; only the 'Farewell' stone survives, built into the left-hand wall.

Wincheap Green

When you negotiate the traffic of the large roundabout today it is hard to visualise the famous Cherry Fair held there and recorded in folk songs. It became so popular that it spilled over all

Martyrs' Memorial. The martyred woman, Alice Benden, had been imprisoned for six weeks in a dungeon known as the 'Monday hole'. Her clothes were so noisome her judge ordered her a bath which also removed her skin.

along Wincheap to the present A2 bypass. Besides fruit and vegetable stalls, wrestling matches were held between white-clad bakers and coal black sweeps and 'bun-biting' competitions where the buns on strings were doused in treacle and the participants' hands tied. Along with other local fairs, in the Precincts, in Longport and St Dunstan's Street, Wincheap's fair went to the cattle market and was combined with a hiring fair. When this way of engaging labourers and servants died out and cattle sales increased, the fair survived, migrating round the edges of town until its demise.

The last burnings at the stake took place on the Green in 1588 when three Roman Catholic priests perished in Armada year. Thereafter forty-one petty thieves were hanged between 1590 and 1593, as large a number as the burned Protestant martyrs of 1555-58. Good trade flourished on these occasions at several inns round the Green. The Wheatsheaf became the Railway Tavern and Hotel in 1862 when the East Station was built; it is at present closed.

On a bare field off Wincheap the ten women and thirty-one men who became Protestant martyrs had suffered. They are all listed on the monument erected in 1899 in nearby **Martyrs' Field Road.** The inscription reads 'For themselves they earned a martyr's crown. By their heroic fidelity they helped to secure for future generations the priceless blessing of religious freedom'. Only in the late nineteenth century were houses built there and within recent memory people recalled visits in childhood to see the stumps of stakes with chains attached and a blackened skull still bearing hair. John Bland, the vicar of Adisham, was burnt praying aloud with three others in a single fire in 1555; the last four burnings were rushed through only two days before Queen Mary's death in 1558. John Foxe's *Book of Martyrs* of 1570 immortalised among others the humble people from the Weald, Ashford and Hythe who died heroically; many households into my own childhood still owned a copy. He told of Alice Snoth, whose name appears on the monument, who recited the catechism, calling on her godparents to attest to her accuracy. 'Then I die a Christian woman,' she called out from the flames. Archbishop Cranmer, under house arrest at the Deanery before his own burning, would have heard the sounds and smelt the stench.

Wincheap was recorded as a wine market in 1200 and a number of its houses hide fifteenth-century timber buildings behind their modernised facades. These hall-houses were extended and adapted into the nineteenth century, for the population grew and migrated rapidly as incomers came to get a foothold in the city. Poor law records reveal multiple occupancy and a lot of poverty alongside flourishing businesses. The Maiden's Head inn on the corner of a modern industrial estate began in the early 1400s, tacked on a free-standing old market hall of about 1500 to be turned into a brew house and then put in a first floor in the 1600s when it became the inn it still is, although in an unstable condition.

Castle Street

This, the main artery of the town in Roman times and the processional way to the cathedral in earlier Saxon centuries, was replaced by the present High Street from Westgate to St George's Gate from the 900s. Before the Black Death this was a poor overcrowded area full of families evicted by the creation of the two castles. The only vestiges of the vanished parishes, both joined to St Mildred's before 1400, are St John's and St Mary's Lanes. The White Hart Inn stands on the site of St Mary's; its churchyard survives as a small public garden. The graveyard continued to house burials from inner city parishes in the High Street and Burgate. In 1842 Dr Rigden of the Canterbury Dispensary blamed such city graveyards as the prime cause of sickness and water pollution. Piped water and an out-of-town cemetery followed within thirty years.

Castle Street contains fine Georgian-seeming houses mostly with late medieval origins. The most notable is number five (Pentin's), the home of **William Somner,** our first historian. His father, Registrar of the Consistory Court, worked from home and kept the records there so

Somner's house. William Somner spent his whole life here. His biographer said, 'His visits within the city were to find the Ancestors rather than the present inhabitants and to know the genealogy of houses, walls and dust'. I wish I were half as good a historian as him.

William, his youngest son and eventual successor, grew up breathing old documents and was helped by Archbishop Laud and by a canon who taught him Anglo-Saxon. His *Antiquities of Canterbury* of 1640, dedicated to Laud, recorded just in time the vanished churches and the glories of the cathedral. He was outraged when the Puritan minister, Richard Culmer, boasted of using 'Mr Somner's great book as a compass to guide me by in that great ocean of images', when in 1643 he destroyed stained glass and beheaded statues there. Somner did salvage the font, hid its pieces and rejoiced in having his son baptized in it in 1660 when it was restored. Friends backed his antiquarian writings under the Commonwealth, he presented Charles II with his *Antiquities* in 1660, got his job back and laboured to restore the library and fabric of the cathedral. His monument in St Margaret's Church lies behind the scenery of *The Canterbury Tales* attraction.

The Free Churches

Presbyterians and Congregationalists were the first two nonconformist sects to set up in Canterbury during the Civil War in the 1640s. They were soon followed by Baptists and Quakers who maintained their separate identities. By the 1790s, when John Wesley's annual visits were fuelling the growth of Methodism, the two first comers were sharing ministers and premises behind what is now the Beaney Institute. They built a joint church in the new Guildhall Street which is now part of Debenhams. Meanwhile a group of Methodists, the Countess of Huntingdon's Connection, had built a church in Watling Street, which was destroyed by bombing in 1942. St Andrew's Church replaced it in a pleasant modern style, housing the old partners as the United Reformed Church until the latest Whitefriars development swept it away. Their new church further down Watling Street boasts Canterbury's first dome.

The Three Tuns inn, existing since the 1500s on the corner of Castle and Watling Streets, is just one of the buildings erected over the **Roman Theatre.** Further foundations lie below the HaHa bar and adjoining estate agents in St Margaret's Street. One of only four theatres found in Britain, its second rebuilding in the early 200s made it an imposing stone, D-shaped showpiece of 71m x 60m, seating 6,000. It was as dominant in the Roman city as the cathedral is today. Sited opposite the temple, it would have staged processions with music and dance as well as plays. The original line of Watling Street was diverted by early Saxon settlers to reach the new market and clusters of huts round the theatre ruins, which archaeologists revealed in the 1970s. Kings like Ethelbert are thought to have used it for occasional folk gatherings. It certainly remained the principal quarry when only chalk and flint were otherwise available. Huge worked stones were found supporting the Saxon cathedral's western apse of the 1020s and rubble from the theatre filled the four Norman piers still supporting Bell Harry Tower.

St Margaret's Street traverses the heart of the Roman city for a huge baths complex, frequently remodelled, has been traced below St Margaret's Church and the Marlowe Arcade and Waterstone's opposite. The basement there contains a viewable fragment of the heated hall where digging revealed the hypocaust system, wall flues and stoke holes. Squatters settled there from the 400s.

St Margaret's Church in this wide market street became the city church where five mayors and other local worthies are buried. It is recorded in 1153 but after the Reformation served also as the Archdeacon's Court where Robert Cushman was tried (see page 39). In 1771 it suffered the indignity of having its chancel lopped off to enable stage coaches to swing into the famous Royal Fountain Hotel opposite where everyone important stayed from King Harold's mother to Queen Victoria. George Gilbert Scott created the shallow flint-clad apse in 1850 when the church interior was Victorianised. The Fountain was destroyed and the church badly damaged in the Blitz of June 1942. After twenty-five years as a church for the deaf it became in 1986 *The Canterbury Tales* attraction. Using the church's height the walkway enables visitors to travel from the Tabard, Southwark, to Becket's shrine, hearing several tales in a number of languages.

The elegant Grecian façade of the **Whitstable Fish Market** was erected in 1822, part of a determined effort to transform a smelly market town into a prosperous and fashionable centre after the Napoleonic Wars. The fish market beside the church had flourished since 1480 when a cartload of oysters paid 1d toll. It was but one of the specialist markets for cloth, salt, rushes, meat, bread and fodder which sprang up in various parts of the town once the 1448 charter allowed the city to collect tolls; the medieval housewife would envy us the supermarket.

United Reformed Church. This twenty-first-century church stands directly on Roman Watling Street at the point where the Saxon settlers diverted its route towards the theatre as today's curve suggests.

Roman city centre. After AD 100 the civilian city was laid out on four central islands. Behind the theatre was the Temple precinct; beside it the Baths complex. The Forum and Basilica lie unexcavated beneath 'Abode' hotel and the Beaney Institute.

Fish market. A cafe/takeaway occupies this site adjoining a popular fish and chip shop patronised by parties visiting *The Canterbury Tales* in the church beyond.

Opposite: Pilgrim inns. This reconstruction drawing is the fruit of several building recordings by the Canterbury Archaeological Trust and shows the inns mentioned in the text.

The busy crossroads where St Margaret's Street meets Mercery Lane and the Parade was the site of Simmons' Canterbury Bank; its Victorian successor is Lloyds. Standing here you can easily conjure up the crowds, noise, dirt and smell of Chaucer's Canterbury. The modern scene of street-traders, buskers, school parties, litter bins and fast food is not so different. Across the street the little Swatch shop gives no idea of the monster building of which it was once the corner. Until the fire of 1865 the three-storeyed courtyard inn **The Cheker of the Hope** stretched down to Nationwide and back halfway down Mercery Lane. Compared to the shops, houses and stalls around it, it seemed as huge then as our new Whitefriars shopping development does today. Built in Chaucer's last days, it was the setting for bawdy parts of *The Tale of Beryn,* a sequel to *The Canterbury Tales.* Thomas Chillenden, the powerful prior (see page 30), realized that monastic hospitality was overstretched and that an inn could be another three-fold money-spinner. Built in three years at a cost of £847 14s 4d it opened in 1392. By turning their shutters into street counters with awnings, the lessees of ground floor lock-up shops could sell goods from workshops inside, using materials stored in the cellars below. Staircases between the shops led wealthy pilgrims up to the first floor to rent grand suites named The White Hart, King's Chamber, or St George's Chamber. Gilded windows on the galleried inner courtyard survive in the rear of Mercery Lane shops. More stairs accessed the vast dormitory sleeping 100 poorer pilgrims under its rafters. Cellar gratings, traceried windows and doorways are all visible in Mercery Lane. Elizabethan travelling players like Lord Leicester's men visited annually to perform in the inn yard until banned by the Puritan city council as 'displeasing to God and to the good quiet of the city'. By then young Christopher Marlowe had had six chances to fuel his passion for the theatre.

The Crown Inn lay between the Cheker and the Buttermarket and forms part of Debenhams; the inn's cellars are now part of its Crypt Restaurant. Starbucks by Christ Church Gate was the Sun tavern erected by the priory in 1437/8; much of its structure remains in the 'Cathedral Gate Hotel' above and in the neighbouring jewellers. The priory owned four more inns in Burgate; the largest was the Bull Inn, rebuilt in timber in the 1430s on the site of a 'great stone house' of the priory dating from 1200. Part of its courtyard can be seen off Butchery Lane and Black's shop on the corner shows clearly how the lock-up shops traded, with lodgings above. The staircases resemble the contemporary arrangements of Oxbridge colleges and the Inns of Court.

On the opposite corner of Mercery Lane stands a building which for the last seventy-five years was Boots. It was in a bad state when they acquired it but in 1931 their own architect rescued and restored it, providing its present approximately fifteenth-century appearance. Perhaps the original corner dragon-post is the only visible external feature of the three shops existing in the 1100s. In time Boots expanded down Mercery Lane, absorbing behind its Georgian façade a three-storey house with its surviving fourteenth-century roof. Boots also extended along the Parade as this part of the High Street is called. In the 1950s they once again carefully unified the frontages to match their original site, changing the windows and plastering the upper storeys. Although the creation of unimpeded floor space swept away other medieval features, below ground lie wonderful early flint-walled vaulted cellars and under one, 4.5m below the street, is a deeper cellar still of the 1300s.

Soloman the Mercer in the 1100s rented this prestigious building from Christ Church Priory at £1 for the house and 13s 6d for the cellar. For over a century after 1700 it became a bookshop catering for the clergy and professionals of a cathedral city. Its last occupant before Boots was Thomas Becket Jewellers and a teashop.

Boots building. The original windows and cellars of the Cheker are visible on the left, while the street scene would strike Chaucer as familiar.

Queen Elizabeth's guest chamber has a fine plaster ceiling upstairs. Plaster decoration like the pargetting on the exterior was a Kentish speciality in the 1600s.

Unlike the gradual accretion of Boots, a purpose-built monster of 1377 occupies the third or south-eastern corner opposite on this important crossroads in the heart of the city. Christ Church Priory planned an investment property stretching 14m down St Margaret's Street and 13m along the Parade to house businesses with shops below and living space above. The Dean and Chapter, succeeding the priory, continued to reap a handsome rental income from the ironmongers and drapers who rented parts of this huge building in steady succession. They altered the internal layout frequently; a handsome Georgian town house with oriel windows was created in the most southerly property. 'Next' turned the ground floor levels into open shop floors before, like Boots, relocating in 2005 to the Whitefriars Precinct.

Queen Elizabeth's Guest Chamber survived the blitz of 1942 when its contemporaries to the east perished. It is now the grandest sixteenth-century timber-framed house inside the walls although its exterior is a century later, with pargetting showing putti frolicking among grapevines and plaster rusticated masonry below. Queen Elizabeth spent a well-recorded three days here for her fortieth birthday in 1574 but there is no evidence for the story that she entertained a French royal suitor here.

The small forecourt to Nason's store was the Church of St Mary Bredman before which the bread market was held. A middle row existed in the Middle Ages further up the street where

The Beaney Institute. The mosaic floor inside and the timber and tesserae of the exterior were designed as an echo of the Roman market and law court on which it stands. It replaced the Coach and Horses inn featured in many old prints.

St Andrew's Church similarly hosted a fish market. It was moved here from St Mary 'Fishman' in Burgate on mayoral orders.

Modern conservationists deplore the priorities of the post-war city council. Their aim was to pull down old slum cottages, build council estates and fine new schools and not spend money on restoring damaged monuments like St George's Church and the city's **ancient Guildhall.** A plaque on Costa Coffee shop on the corner of Guildhall Street is the sole reminder of a building 'recently rebuilt' when the city received its Charter in 1448. Weekly law courts and fortnightly council meetings continued until 1942 and in 1950 the Guildhall was demolished as too expensive to repair (see page 54 for the new Guildhall). Until 1885 Canterbury returned two MP's elected at open hustings at the Buttermarket and the Guildhall. The most dramatic scene there was in 1832 when 'Sir William Courteney, Knight of Malta', alias a Cornishman John Nichol Tom, dressed in a gold-trimmed Tudor crimson velvet suit, standing on a table waved his sword demanding annual elections and 'votes for all over eighteen'. He was eventually killed in Bossenden Wood near Boughton in 1838 leading the last English labourers' revolt sparked by the hated new Poor Law. In 1852 a Royal Commission sat for eleven days at the Guildhall investigating corrupt election practices. As a result Canterbury was disfranchised from 1852-54 and again from 1880-82 for a system issuing coloured tickets redeemable for 50p if you voted 'correctly'.

On the site of the old Coach and Horses inn stands the strange monument to the hard struggles of one of the city's most colourful native sons. This is the eye-catching exuberance of **the Beaney Institute**, our library and museum.

James George Beaney (1828-91) worked as a grocer's assistant until he caught the attention of Dr Rigden of the Canterbury Dispensary. He trained him in pharmacy, taught him Latin and financed him through medical training at Edinburgh University. After a chequered career on emigrant ships, in the Crimean War and at a failed Canterbury pharmacy, he ended up with a doctor's practice in gold-rush Melbourne. He cut such a dash that he was nicknamed 'Diamond Jimmy' for the rings he wore over his hogskin gloves. Jealous rivals took him to court in a series of scandals relating to bribery, plagiarism, back-street abortion and the deaths of patients under surgery. He survived to be elected to the Legislative Council of Victoria and died worth £60,000. The city council received £10,000 for the 'Beaney Institute for the Education of the labouring Man'; the cathedral £1,000 for a nave monument depicting the Good Samaritan; his indigent brother got £10 and his pauper sister nothing.

The building now houses the KCC public library and the City Museum's Art Gallery. Both bodies plan an ambitious extension with a Heritage Lottery Fund grant which will encroach on what was Dancing School Yard and a non-conformist chapel. It is thought to have been the site of Sir Thomas More's house on the site of the Roman Basilica and Forum. Unfortunately, modern piling techniques will not allow for much archaeology on this central site, the lost quarter of the Roman city.

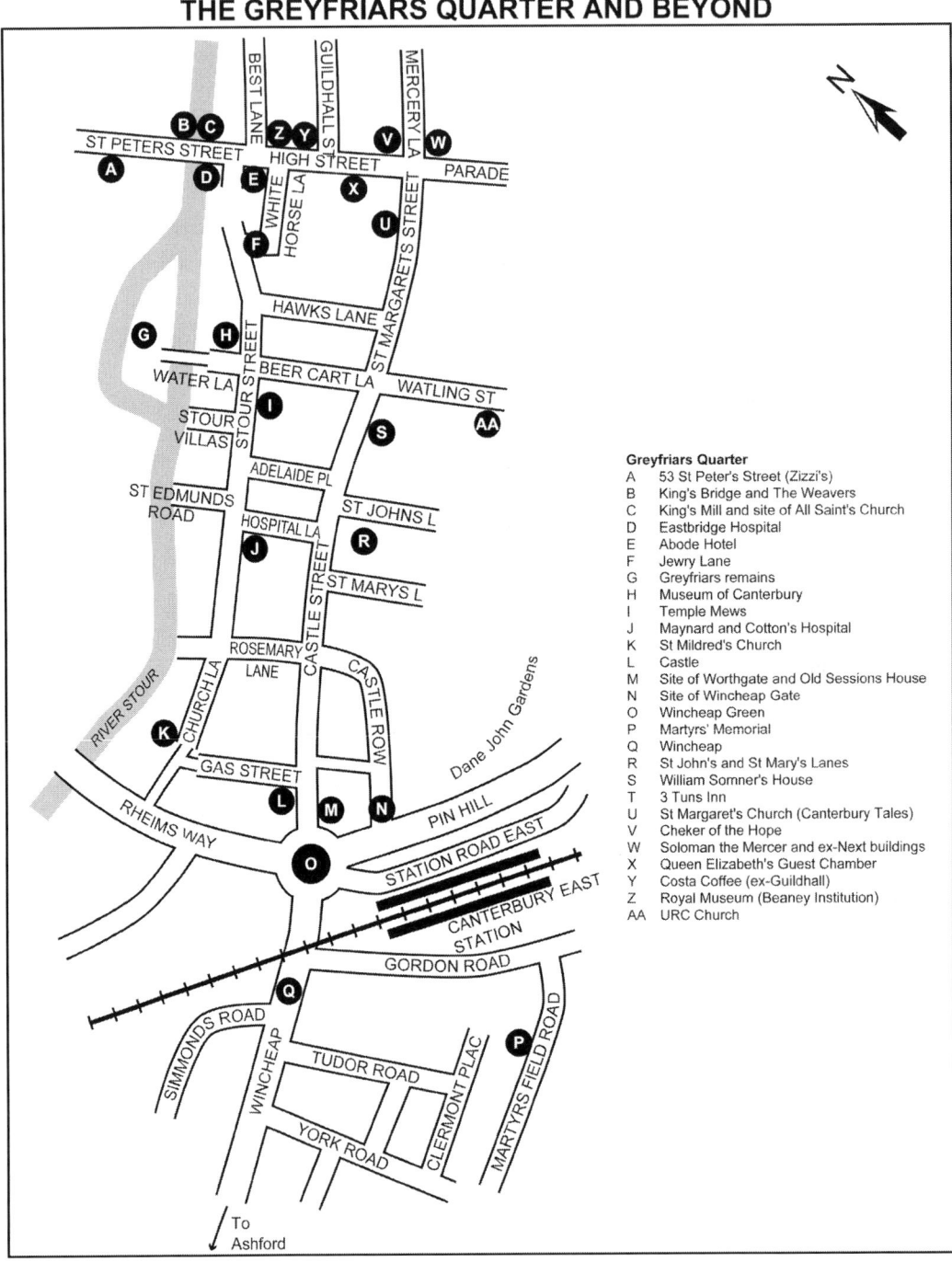

Five
The Whitefriars Quarter

The Canterbury Blitz 1942 and after
Pre-war Canterbury was a typical small market and cathedral town with its cattle market and four cinemas, its year punctuated by Cricket Week at the St Lawrence Ground and, from 1928, the Cathedral Festival plays. In 1939 the city actually received evacuees who were moved on when France fell, an exodus augmented by the cathedral choristers and other school parties. An order arrived that in case of invasion the Home Guard should man the ancient city walls to the end. The devastating effect of incendiary bombs on a close-packed medieval city was demonstrated in the 'Baedeker' raid on Exeter in April 1942 but, following the allied 1,000 bomber raid on Cologne, it was Canterbury's turn.

On the night of 1 June, the flares dropped to pinpoint the cathedral drifted on the wind from the coast to settle on the top end of town, particularly on St George's parish. Then, for one-and-a-half hours, 100 high-explosive and thousands of incendiary bombs rained on the city. On the cathedral roof, a team of fire-watchers tossed the incendiaries on to the grass below. The principal loss was the cathedral Library where the valuable books had already been removed. Other buildings in the Precincts were damaged, including the Deanery. Only forty-eight people lost their lives that night but, in the city two churches, the Corn Exchange, the Longmarket most of the Simon Langton Grammar Schools and many timber-framed medieval houses were lost. By the end of the war, 10,445 bombs dropped in 135 separate raids had killed 115 people and destroyed over 900 homes and public buildings. The demolition did not end here, however.

Even before the war the Labour housing minister, George Lansbury, when praising the council's ambitious slum clearance programme of 1,000 houses in ten years, had forecast that every unfit house would go. After the war rows of cottages in ancient lanes were demolished, only to be replaced some fifty years later with pastiche copies, suitable for today's single households. From 1948 to 1974 buildings deemed too damaged or to have outlived their purpose came down; we lost the Guildhall, St George's Terrace and Church and the Fleur de Lys Inn. The 1945 Holden Plan aimed to divert traffic and create cathedral vistas in a radical plan involving a new road parallel to the High Street and the compulsory purchase of seventy-five central acres.

As after the Great Fire of London, the ratepayers revolted; they wanted their houses and shops quickly rebuilt within their ancient boundaries. When the Citizens' Defence Association won the next Council elections, shops in 'contemporary' style sprang up on the thirty-five acres the council bought. Much land lay open as surface car parks or stretches of willow herb or buddleia. New council estates and schools and the beginning of a city ring road absorbed the council's energy and budget. Only in the mid-1970s, when tourism had become a major source of income, did a change of heart occur and Conservation became the buzz-word.

Looking eastwards up the main street from Butchery Lane, nearly everything behind you is old and almost all before you dates from the last sixty years. As a visiting schoolgirl in 1938 my impression was of a narrow, traffic-clogged street of tall, dark buildings up to St George's Church. As a student I revisited the blitzed city in 1944 and 1945. Apart from the façade of Marks &

The Corn Exchange. The Corn and Hop Exchange was the most imposing late eighteenth-century building in Canterbury. It and the Longmarket bore the brunt of the bombs missing the Cathedral in June 1942.

Opposite: Bombs on Canterbury. This plots all the wartime incidents. After the two principal raids in 1942 some German bombers failing to reach London unloaded their cargoes here; others are failed V1 and V2 rockets

2 Mad Henry of Fordwich, beaten by his
to Becket's Tomb, is healed (Trinity Chape
side). (Dean and Chapter of Canterbury C

3 Bossanyi's Salvation window of 1958 (so
east transept). (Dean and Chapter of Cant
Cathedral)

6 Christ Church Gate. Prince Arthur and Katharine of Aragon's arms flank the Beaufort portcullis and the Tudor Rose. The Royal arms are supported by the Welsh dragon and Lancastrian whippet.

7 Prior Goldstone's pun on his name surmounts the pedestrian gate.

9 St Alphege. Canterbury besiege Alphege taken by boat to Greenw killed. (Thirteenth-century glass North Quire Ambulatory

10 Conquest House. Rear of No stone house with later timber ad the four knights assembled here b Becket's murder. (Palace Street)

13 John Thomas, point maker, installed this panelling in 1529 when altering Cokyn's old h
(Zizzi's Restaurant)

Above: Longmarket dig. This central site encouraged the Archaeological Trust to provide its first raised walkway to inform school parties and the public about the evolving discoveries. Working with Land Securities, the educational opportunities the trust offered would expand in two further major developments.

Right: Butchery Lane. Unlike York, trades were not concentrated in specific areas except here and in neighbouring Mercery Lane. Specific markets were scattered across the city.

Opposite above: After the blitz. This dramatic aerial view shows how the enemy flares drifting on the wind concentrated the bombs on a wide area south of the Cathedral.

Opposite below: 'The Shoe Box' was the nickname given to this post-war building on the Longmarket site. The square and Cathedral view were appreciated; the latest rebuild has kept the first and lost the second.

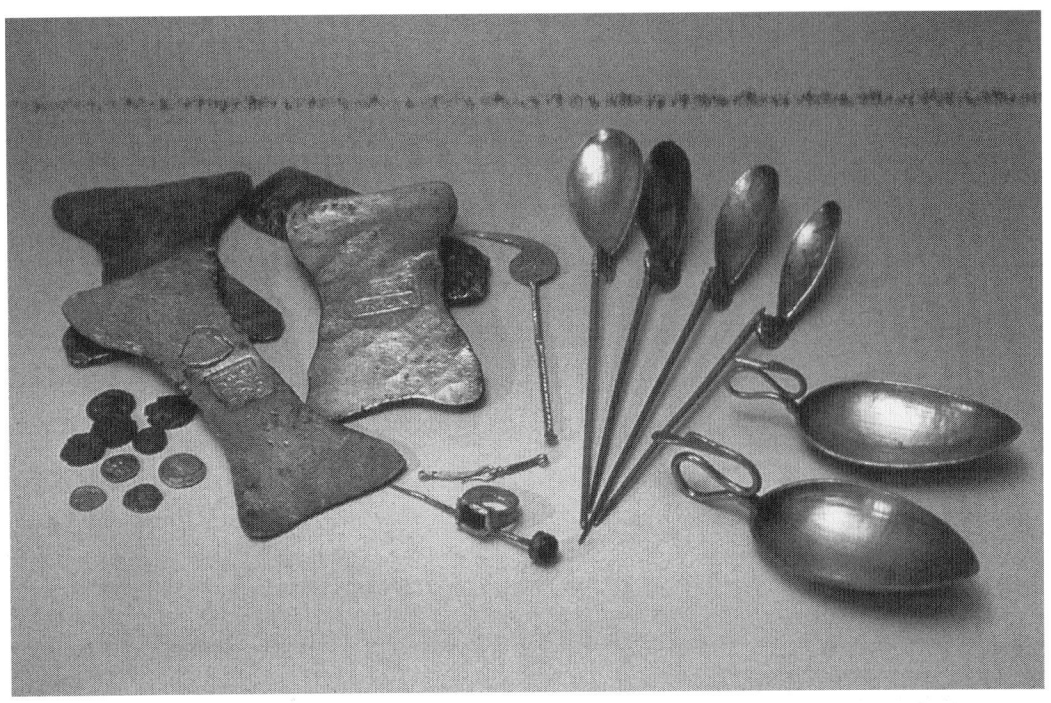

Roman silver hoard. This treasure trove of AD 410 in the museum is solid proof of a Christian community in the Roman city. The central *ligula* and two spoons bear Christian symbols.

Spencer I saw a bombed desert dotted with placards advertising the present whereabouts of vanished shops. In the ruins the first volunteer archaeologists were already at work in cellars where they would later find the Roman mosaics now part of the underground Roman Museum, a Roman bathhouse on the Woolworth's site and the ground plans of homes of every age from the Saxons onwards. The open space of the **Longmarket** had once been occupied by the Corn Exchange and a long market hall stretching back to Burgate. The first post-war development created the square which protestors managed to retain during planning battles before the 1980s creations in large pastiche which you see today. The excavations preceding this rebuild uncovered the heart of the booming Norman city with its twelve goldsmiths, eight mints, its 200 lock-up shops and Jewish money-lenders. The wealthy, like Theoric the Goldsmith and Sunwin the Smith, chose to cluster in this higher and healthier end of town. What the archaeologists found exactly matched the voluminous cathedral rent-rolls which were the basis for Dr William Urry's *Canterbury under the Norman and Angevin Kings* with its earliest detailed maps of a medieval English town. Even Theoric's smelting crucibles were found in his workshop. **Butchery Lane** itself was once a smelly place with its Shambles for offal scavenged by the town's animals from 6 p.m. to curfew. One bull's head remains over what is now a shoe-mender's shop. Opposite are the pinched Ionic columns leading down to the Roman Museum. Bombed in the war and part-burnt in the 1990s the rest of the lane is mostly modern restoration. It was once called Angel Lane from the angel on the cathedral south-west gable framed at the end of the lane. Before you reach Burgate lies the entrance to what remains of the yard of the Bull Inn and on its corner is the best impression of what the Inn looked like, restored with archaeological advice in the 1980s.

St Mary Magdalene Tower is all that remains of 'St Mary Fishman'. Richard Harris Barham of *Ingoldsby Legends* fame was baptised here. St Thomas' RC church lies behind and contains two Becket relics.

Old Burgate. This sixteenth-century reconstruction shows the guard chamber adapted as living quarters and the city ditch surviving since Roman times.

Zoar Chapel was occupied by the Strict and Particular Baptists from 1845 once piped water came to this end of the town and the cisterns were removed.

Burgate

Turning right up Burgate you are in a very ancient street. The tower of **St Mary Magdalene** Church (1503), with its fine restored monument inside, survived the demolition of the church in 1871. The fish market for the priory and the Abbey was held here, hence the church's popular name 'St Mary Fishman.' Riots during which a canon was slapped round the face with a halibut occurred when the mayor proposed moving the market to the High Street. The Roman Catholic Church of St Thomas now stands beside the tower. The bombed shops on the cathedral side of Burgate were rebuilt by the Dean and Chapter, aided by a generous grant from Canada. It is thought that the line of Burgate formed part of the staked defences to the 'burh' or stronghold where the early Saxon kings maintained a hall, defended on two other sides by the Roman walls. This high ground gave the city its modern name 'Cant-wara-burh', the Kentish people's stronghold. It is, of course, now the cathedral and its precinct. Passing a few remaining older houses, including No. 61, once the home of Richard Harris Barham of the *Ingoldsby Legends*, you reach the site of **Burgate itself**, outlined in the pavement. The old

St George's Tower. At 2.18 a.m. on 2 June 1942 flames reached the Victorian clock to mark the end of a church of 1164 which, though reparable, was demolished. The Norman tower remains with its famous clock though without its wooden spire. Avery Sabine and the last prioress of St Sepulchre's nunnery were among famous Canterburians buried here; only Marlowe's baptism is commemorated.

dual carriageway Roman gate to Richborough Fort became a main gate to the Saxon borough and was rebuilt during the refortification of the city walls in 1475. This partly brick gate with a drawbridge and side towers was converted above into lodgings. St Michael's Church which began above the gate had long been resited on the north side. One stone remained embedded in the wall when the gate came down in stages between 1781 and 1822. Outside the wall on the south side was the very fine Saracen's Head Inn which fell victim to the present ring road; some of its salvaged timbers can be seen in the roof of Eastbridge Hospital Chapel (see page 68). Burgate marked the limit of the city's responsibility for the fifteenth-century modernisation of the defensive walls; the cathedral priory's work begins here, best seen in the adjoining Broad Street car park. The various brick intrusions belonged to houses, such as our first doctor's surgery, swept away for the ring road.

Burgate Lane inside the walls to the right was created as the earth bank behind the wall was gradually carted off for gardens and cesspits. The bastion which is now the Zoar Baptist Chapel received its brick cladding to contain the city water cisterns when St George's Gate was demolished in 1801. Its drum towers had held the cisterns for this end of town once Archbishop Abbot's Conduit together with St Andrew's Church in the High Street fell to the eighteenth-century improvers. In 1643 Baptists had been the first non-conformist sect to strike root in the

St George's Gate. This picture shows the soldiers who kept permanent guard on the military stores held in the tower until 1801. They were commonly said to have been very fresh with passing ladies. (Canterbury Royal Museum & Art Gallery Copyright reserved 2007 ©)

city and had their later chapel at Blackfriars. Their heated internal debates and prohibitions on 'marrying out' created Unitarian and other splinter groups. Today's busy Baptist Church is in New Dover Road.

Where this lane joins the main street there is no old 'history you can see', except **St George's Tower**, but instead three phases of recent history – the redevelopments of the 1950s, a modernist phase of 1965 to 1980, and the period since the Millennium. **St George's Gate**, excavated in 1988 ahead of the modern roundabout, was first called Newingate when it was created in the Roman wall about AD 900. The gate, rebuilt between 1483 and 1495 was based on the Westgate and had drum towers. Since its carriageway was only 7ft wide it came down in 1801, part of the scheme to modernise the Saxon cattle market beyond and create a weighbridge. When Christopher Marlowe grew up here in the 1560s/1570s, the gate was kept and occupied as a charity by Widow Sweeting and her family. Her husband, the ex-parish clerk and the vicar of St George's, had died so poor he could only leave a groat (2p) to each of his children; young Len Sweeting was a fellow-scholar of Christopher's at the King's School. St George's parish in their day was the noisiest and smelliest in town as animals were driven from the market outside to Butchery Lane past the Marlowe cobbler's shop. Christopher, the oldest of six surviving children was baptised in the church opposite in February 1564. Both church and shop were

The 1950s colonnade has survived later rebuilds partly because its covered walkway remains popular especially when a bi-weekly market fills the street.

heavily bombed in 1942 and when the decision was made to demolish the church the tower was retained with a plaque commemorating Marlowe. A recent application for an ice-cream kiosk beneath it was rejected but it stands unsullied amidst its modern neighbours and a bi-weekly street market. The Marlowe's shop lay below Fenwick's (2003) whose tower-like east end is a pale pastiche of the old gate. The site of Wilkinson's opposite was occupied in the 1100s by a moneyer, William, son of Winedi; a William the Conqueror penny of 1087 minted by his father was found below the shop.

Looking down the pedestrianised part of St George's Street you see the 1930s Marks & Spencer's, the sole survivor of the blitz, and the 1950s era of postwar rebuilding, dominant in the terrace of shops with their colonnade of 1952-1955, built to the old scale for a city of small shops. Superdrug on the opposite side next to Woolworth's won the original owner, the grocery chain David Greig, a prize for post-war design in 1956.

When the bus station moved to its present position and the Simon Langton boys' school finally vacated their bomb-damaged Whitefriars site in 1959 a new wave of modernism overtook

David Greig's and Superdrug, its successor, stands over a late Roman bathhouse excavated after the war by Sheppard Frere. It was important for setting a dating plan for earlier centuries. In its last years a gaming room seems to have occupied an old bath.

the planners. Old roads were greatly widened, old houses in the way were removed and the first encroachment on the Whitefriars was Riceman's, a huge brick, deep-cellared department store, the first out-of-scale monster completed in 1962. In 1968, after fierce opposition which succeeded in cutting off one layer only, the detested concrete multi-storey car park was erected over an old graveyard behind Riceman's. On the redundant surface car park further large concrete developments followed through the 1970s including a Whitefriars shopping centre accessed by a bridge over Rose Lane. This centre destroyed the remaining above-ground vestiges of the Whitefriars' Church and precinct wall. These buildings appear in the aerial view on page 89.

Today the legacy of this era is only those widened roads misnamed St George's and Rose 'Lanes' and the continuing pressure to build on a large scale, for the tide turned in the 1980s. Land Securities' developments at the Longmarket and behind St George's Church reverted to pitched roofs and a mixture of old styles, which some like no better than the concrete.

The Big Dig

Canterbury Archaeological Trust had conducted city digs, open to the public, at both these sites, following experience gained at digs across the post-war Marlowe car parks off St Margaret's Street. This third rebuilding of the Whitefriars area from 1999 to 2004 was to be their biggest challenge. Over 100 diggers spent these five years in all weathers at six sites, under tight time pressures, to explore one seventh of the city. It was the biggest urban excavation in Britain and produced 35 tons of material, still being analysed. The Trust, true to its founding principle, 'the education of the public in archaeology', enabled 46,617 people to experience and learn from

Left: St Augustine's Abbey stones. Excavations in St George's Street discovered that a Tudor builder acquired these stones cheaply, carved in 1200 for the Abbey, to be bases for the corner posts of his house. They spent over four hundred years below ground before being seen by visitors to the Big Dig in 2002.

Below: The Big Dig. Where Fenwick's now stands the excavation has exposed Roman, Saxon and Whitefriars remains viewed from a walkway connected to the museum and shop.

Above: School visit. Teachers in consultation with the CAT's education officer planned during preliminary visits tailor-made worksheets for students from primary to university age.

Right: The *bulla* of Nicholas V (1147-55). Indulgences releasing the payer from present or future sins were fund-raisers for Roman papal building works. St Peter is shown bearded and St Paul bald.

Simon Langton Boys' School. This pre-war parade shows the 1880s buildings before the blitz. Until 1959 parts of the Whitefriars gate and a wall survived among the pre-fabs and repaired classrooms. Known as the 'front line school' it was nearest to Nazi Europe. The girls' half was so damaged they moved out in 1942.

these excavations. A Titan portacabin was museum, shop and visitor centre and the Friends of the Trust provided seven-day guiding on the walkways, the volunteers being briefed every week by the experts. Finds days, school visits, after-work talks and a 'Little Dig' for children were some of the ways the facilities were expanded. Financial aid came first from *Time Team* and then from the Heritage Lottery Fund.

Since this was to be the third disturbance of the area expectations were not high, especially in the region of the Whitefriars' cloister where Riceman's basement had penetrated deep. Although finds were fragmentary, much stone had been robbed and foundations cut by later wells and pits, a picture of this area is now emerging. It was always on the edge of the Roman city and was never fully developed up to the line of their eastern walls of 270 to 290. Wooden houses begin to appear on the western limits in the second century to be followed by larger stone houses, continually improved. A fine corridor house had heated rooms and mosaics, its inhabitants used a range of imported pottery and one seems to have been a coin collector. There was some evidence for sub-Roman life of a hand-to-mouth sort continuing into the 400s and for a few Saxon sunken huts and hearths but the area seems to have been largely abandoned until the 900s. When the High Street and its Newingate then arrived, a series of lanes grew running off a service lane behind the High Street shops. These filled up with the humble houses and workshops of small traders. In the 1340s eighteen Augustinian Whitefriars arrived to squat behind the cloth market, refusing tithes to the vicar and rent to the priory. After the ravages of the Black Death it was even easier to extend their precinct over the old craftsmen's area (see colour plate 12). Despite modern damage, parts of their kitchen and warming room, the north wall of their church and their vast

Roman internal tower. Although cleaned out in this picture, the tower was solid and helped to confirm the date of our Roman walls to 270-90, the period when the 'Saxon Shore' forts were being modernised.

5m-deep cess tank were found, although little in the cloisters. They had become patrons of the city trade associations who kept altars in their church which was also embellished by wealthy legal families. Their number had dwindled by the 1530s and they were accused of all-night drinking and gambling. One find was an Indulgence Bull or seal of Pope Nicholas V bearing the heads of Saints Peter and Paul. Such indulgences later incensed Martin Luther in Germany. One heroic Whitefriar redeemed their reputation in 1538. In front of Richard Ingworth, who had already dissolved the Black and Grey Friars in the previous two days, Father John Stone asserted 'There can be no head of the Church but God and I will die for it'. 'And so you shall', replied Ingworth sending him for interrogation to the Tower of London and later imprisonment in Canterbury Castle and the Westgate. His grisly end came on the Dane John Mound where he was hanged, disembowelled, quartered and his parts parboiled for display on the city gates. City accounts record 2d for 'the woman who scoured out the cauldron' and '6d for a lamb for Mr Mayor when the Justices did sit on Father Stone'. He was canonised by Pope John Paul II.

The Whitefriars Precinct became a private house, once occupied by Mrs Knight, an aunt of Jane Austen's brother, with whom she took tea on her Canterbury visits. It became the home of the Canterbury Middle Schools for Boys and Girls in 1881. The separated buildings were part-financed by closing the old charity and apprentice schools and amalgamating their endowments. Heavily bombed in 1942 the girls had to move out at once but until 1959 the boys' grammar school continued in the remaining buildings and huts, where ink froze during winter terms. Both grammar schools flourish on new sites since Kent has so far maintained a selective entry system.

The Cattlemarket. The wall where auctioneers' offices burrowed in was reconstructed when the present ring road obliterated the age-old market.

The wall-walk continues southwards above the new bus station passing a cycle facility recently opened where excavation revealed an internal Roman tower probably used as a platform for a catapult; display boards explain what was found. Before the war a row of fine Regency and Victorian houses, St George's Terrace, fronted by railings overlooked the cattle market which had existed since Saxon times outside the walls. Though gutted in the blitz their demolition was not inevitable. A former resident, Kenneth Pinnock, has given this charming reminiscence of his childhood view. 'My face pressed against the stout railing which ran along the top of what was left of the city wall, I could see almost from end to end of that market. Here was drama indeed; the befuddled sheep forced along predestined paths, the brawny assistants ever alert to the least sign of uncooperativeness, the auctioneers and their clerks sallying forth from their offices, burrowed into the city wall beneath my feet, to reach the rostra and spray their intent audience with a machine-gun fire of bids punctuated by bangs of the gavel.' The city ring road brought the market's long history to a close. It used to spill up Dover Street opposite, a street started in Saxon times as a short cut to St George's Gate from the old Dover Road. It had many pubs to slake the drovers' thirst; the White Horse is a fine survivor among the modern buildings of the ring road. At the top end of Dover Street was the Oaten Hill market and a gallows to which the condemned, ropes round their necks, had walked all the way from the Westgate under a hail of garbage.

Ridingate

It is worth coming down off the wall walk to read the display board below the 1970s bridge. This details the long history of this Roman gate into the city from Dover. The Saxons gave it its name, perhaps 'road-gate', 'reed-gate' or 'red-gate' from the red-brick bonding courses the Romans incorporated into this double-arched gate with its two guard chambers. During excavation in 1986 it was seen how, in the 300s, one carriageway was privatised to be let to a blacksmith. Six feet down, the bottom nails of the wooden gate and its hinge survive from when it was last closed to traffic seven centuries ago, while buses turn, oblivious, into the bus station. In early Norman times a knight Vitalis who features galloping across the Bayeux Tapestry, built St Edmund's Chapel in the near guard chamber. It shut when the Black Death decimated its congregation. The Gate was then nicknamed 'the Dung Cart Gate' where night soil men, who also cleared the muck heaps on the Dane John field, took their dripping loads to sell to farmers outside before returning to a drink in the pub by the gate.

Alderman Simmons, that remover of other city gates, pulled down Ridingate in 1799 and built a brick arched bridge instead as part of his plan for the gardens you reach next along the wall walk. Before and after the Second World War the pioneer *Invicta* locomotive, painted red, stood where the pub had been; it is now restored to its original condition and better housed in the Museum of Canterbury.

The Old Dover Road

The Roman line of Watling Street which the Saxons diverted towards the theatre inside the walls was neglected outside when Dover Street became the easiest route to the Newingate (St George's Gate). Today it leads towards the hospital, new schools and the St Lawrence County Cricket ground, named after St Augustine's Abbey's leper hospital once there. The first stretch of road to the traffic lights led to St Sepulchre's Bar, the outer limit of the city's jurisdiction. Here, in May 1660, the mayor and council greeted home Charles II from exile. The money they gave him was returned to the cathedral at evensong when the King, horrified by the puritan damage of 1643, hoped that the dean would restore the canons' stalls; his arms surmount them today. William Somner had also given him a copy of his *Antiquities of Canterbury* bound in Canterbury leather; history does not record whether he read it. **St Sepulchre's Nunnery** was so thoroughly destroyed that only part of the wall survives opposite St Mary Bredin Church, on the corner of Nunnery Fields Road. The Norman knight Vitalis, a vassal of Odo of Bayeux, was granted the manor on which the modern church stands. His son Hamo also founded St Mary Bredin (or wooden) in the city. He and his sister persuaded St Anselm, the archbishop, to regularise a group of nuns tending a chapel on an ancient Roman graveyard opposite their home. The nunnery thus founded in early crusading days and named after the Holy Sepulchre in Jerusalem was always a poor house of about eight Benedictine nuns. For instance, they were allowed by Richard I to gather firewood in Blean Forest for one day a year using one horse. They gained unwelcome notoriety at the end when two Greyfriars and two cathedral monks sponsored a visionary servant girl, Elizabeth Barton, whom they placed in the nunnery. When she prophesied that Henry VIII would be damned to hell within a year if he divorced Catherine of Aragon the message of the 'Nun of Kent' spread rapidly. Unwise visions against so powerful a monarch, repeated after he had married Ann Boleyn, reaped the rapid and brutal execution of all five at Tyburn on charges of treason. In 1536 the nunnery was the first religious house to be dissolved. To end a sad tale on a happier note, when St Mary Bredin was badly bomb-damaged in 1942 it was rebuilt here on Vitalis' and Hamo's original manor and is a very successful evangelical church.

Dane John Gardens. Diaries and letters from Jane Austen onwards praise this city amenity which has incidentally preserved the best stretch of its medieval walls. The Millennium project has added a fountain and a garden for the blind. (Canterbury Royal Museum & Art Gallery Copyright reserved 2007 ©)

Returning towards Ridingate, Vernon Place and **Vernon Grange**, the castellated villa at its junction with the road on the right, record the gratitude of the artist Sidney Cooper (see page 37) to his first patron after whom he named his home at Harbledown Vernon Holme, now Kent College Junior School. Vernon had made a fortune selling remounts to Wellington during the Peninsular War and bought Cooper's depiction of the battle of Waterloo. Beyond a row of nineteenth-century cottages the Kent and Canterbury Club is a fine Georgian survivor. **The Police Station** was built in the 1960s. Christ Church University is currently rebuilding its neighbour, hoping to incorporate a local studies centre.

The Dane John Gardens

Before the Romans, several mounds existed in this area whether as burials or as markers on salt or other track ways crossing the Stour. Two were flattened for Canterbury East Rail Station in 1862, the truncated remains of another displays secondhand cars on the nearby ring road. Two more have been recorded beneath the fire station and the cinema.

Before Roman Durovernum was walled in 270 the gardens were a cemetery containing our remaining mound. Norman and eighteenth-century alterations still frustrated investigation of the mound's origins during the garden improvements of the Millennium Project of 2000. When the Roman planners left half the original town outside the western walls, they took in this area in compensation, which perhaps provided the defended pasture or allotments allowing some Roman way of life to persist up to 450. Inside Ridingate a possible late livestock market was found.

William the Conqueror, en route from Hastings to his London coronation, ordered a wooden keep to be built on the mound and surrounded by a bailey. When Saxon inhabitants had been driven out, the men were forced to dig a 3m-deep ditch round this bailey using the soil to consolidate the mound. Archaeologists in the 1980s traced the bailey in a figure of eight across the gardens to the nineteenth-century houses and across the ring road near the modern station. All this labour was vain since within thirty years a new castle was built near the river where the successor stone castle still stands. During the middle ages the ditch became a rubbish dump and the pasture a drying ground. When plague struck, huts for the victims created a kind of isolation hospital. Elizabethans used it for maypole dancing, archery practice and occasional duelling.

In 1790 **Alderman Simmons** (see page 67) set about creating his public gardens. Starting at a peppercorn rent from the Council he ended with a rent-free lease for life. In the next five years he spent £1,500 on his transformations. He consolidated the earth ramparts to create the terrace along the walls and filled the round bastions with 'flowering shrubs and commodious seats'. He raised the mound by 18 ft (5.5 m) making serpentine hedged and gravelled walks to the summit which commanded 'uninterrupted views of the city and adjacent country' from the seats on the platform. His great lime avenue 344.5 m in length is still with us. Yet in 1795 Simmons after his vast expenditure was dunned for £8 arrears of poor rate and threw his creation back at the city writing, 'What a return is this! I say to you and the public at large, you are heartily welcome'. The gardens have remained a popular and much-used amenity where Victorian regimental bands once played weekly and order was kept by a uniformed beadle. Its row of fine early nineteenth-century houses are still very desirable residences. A Christmas Euro-market, Japanese kite-flying, beer festivals and pop concerts diversify the award-winning restored gardens today, although more than 'one uniformed beadle' are too often needed to stem modern vandalism which recently lost the gardens their European green flag.

You can still climb the mound, now crowned with Simmons' monument of 1803, provided by a repentant Council. From it you survey not only the Cathedral but what the last sixty years have done with this Whitefriars end of the city.

The City Walls

Now that Simmons' flowering shrubs have gone you can see some of the sixteen open horseshoe towers with which the City re-fortified its section of the walls between 1378 and 1408. They have projecting skirts of ashlar and their gun loops afford fire through 180 degrees. The cathedral priory's eight square bastions on the north and west sections are by contrast old-fashioned. Since the French never mounted an invasion it may all seem a great waste of money, but the French did take over and burn Sandwich in 1449; even today its councillors wear black robes. The dry ditch outside the walls, first created by the Romans, survived as a public garden until the creation of the ring road when the wall was consolidated, the *Invicta* engine moved and the concrete bridge at Ridingate replaced Simmons' brick one.

THE WHITEFRIARS QUARTER AND OUTSIDE THE EASTERN WALLS

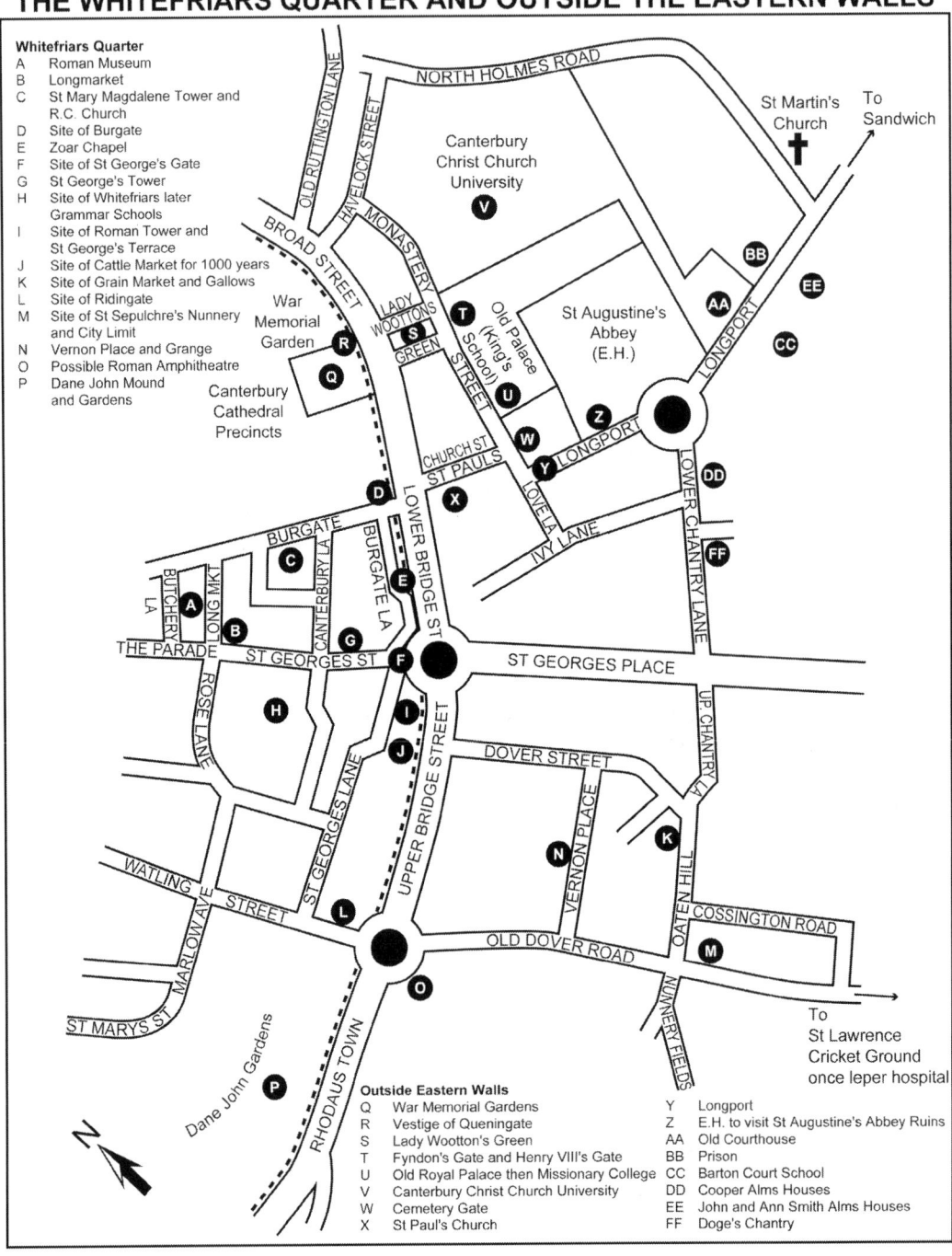

Whitefriars Quarter
- A Roman Museum
- B Longmarket
- C St Mary Magdalene Tower and R.C. Church
- D Site of Burgate
- E Zoar Chapel
- F Site of St George's Gate
- G St George's Tower
- H Site of Whitefriars later Grammar Schools
- I Site of Roman Tower and St George's Terrace
- J Site of Cattle Market for 1000 years
- K Site of Grain Market and Gallows
- L Site of Ridingate
- M Site of St Sepulchre's Nunnery and City Limit
- N Vernon Place and Grange
- O Possible Roman Amphitheatre
- P Dane John Mound and Gardens

Outside Eastern Walls
- Q War Memorial Gardens
- R Vestige of Queningate
- S Lady Wootton's Green
- T Fyndon's Gate and Henry VIII's Gate
- U Old Royal Palace then Missionary College
- V Canterbury Christ Church University
- W Cemetery Gate
- X St Paul's Church
- Y Longport
- Z E.H. to visit St Augustine's Abbey Ruins
- AA Old Courthouse
- BB Prison
- CC Barton Court School
- DD Cooper Alms Houses
- EE John and Ann Smith Alms Houses
- FF Doge's Chantry

six
Outside The Eastern Walls

War Memorial Gardens
At the eastern end of the Precincts, beyond the old cemetery gate, lie the Kent War Memorial Gardens, created after the First World War. The central cross was erected and a bastion of the city wall was converted into a memorial chapel. In the wall beside it is an inscribed stone from the Cloth Hall in Ypres, given by that city in memory of the many Kentish soldiers from the Buffs and the West Kent Regiment who fell in the three battles of Ypres. An annual remembrance service is held during Cricket Week for the dead of both wars and of continuing conflicts. The beautifully kept gardens are a favourite with photographers; the magnificent wisteria along the western wall was planted, so tradition holds, to celebrate the publication of the King James Bible in 1611. Americans remember the descendants of Canon Gookin who lived beside the garden at the time. His son took cattle to Virginia in 1620; his grandson wrote the first history of New England and is buried at Harvard. In the next generation one son became a missionary to the native Indians and the other Governor of Pennsylvania. The missionary's son wrote for seven years the celebrated *Revolutionary Journal* during the War of Independence (see also page 39).

When you are standing in the Broad Street car park, surrounded by vehicles and facing the ring road's non-stop traffic flow, the St Augustine's Abbey complex before you seems divorced from the cathedral and city. Beside the square bastion, once the chapel of St Mary Queningate, you can see the Roman postern gate, embedded in the wall through which Queen Bertha passed in the years before St Augustine's arrival in 597, on her way to St Martin's Church. Queningate preserves her name and Stephen Melton's statues on **Lady Wootton's Green** are the most recent visible reminders of her story and an attempt to link the three parts of the World Heritage Site, despite the traffic.

The Green had a well-recorded market in late Saxon times when a community of craftsmen had been drawn to work for the Abbey. Their traces have been found under the outer domestic court, now the campus of Canterbury Christ Church University. The *Anglo-Saxon Chronicle* accused the abbot of 1011 of treachery when the Vikings stormed and looted the city but left the exposed Abbey and its people alone.

Incendiary bombs in 1942 largely destroyed the houses round the Green. On the left as you face the great gate is the modern face of the rebuilt Abbey Almonry; its thirteenth-century flint walls were found intact to first floor level.

Once the first Norman abbots had rebuilt the church their successors from 1100 to 1276 started on the domestic buildings round the cloister and the surviving guest hall to the right of the gate. The gate and court as you see them today were originally the work of Abbot Fyndon in the nine years from 1300. Extensive abbey lands were producing ample funds to build the Abbot a new great hall, chapel and grand apartments on the east side, a new northern cellarer's range and the gate itself with turrets, crenellations and an upper chamber. When the gate was restored after the war the figure of a monk was added on top. All this accommodation enabled the Abbey to share in the proceeds of the pilgrim trade and entertain the good and the great. By 1538 it was the fourteenth richest English abbey.

War Memorial Chapel. The Ypres stone to the left of the door is now barely decipherable.

Fyndon gate. In 1824 a nineteen-year-old Frenchman, Louis Razé, began publishing his prints of Canterbury by subscription. By his death in 1873 he had fixed a Gothic image of Canterbury in Victorian minds, still affecting modern postcards.

Butterfield Court. This sensitive yet practical restoration showed Butterfield's respect for his medieval predecessors and use of local building tradition in flint and tile.

Some of these splendid buildings survived Henry VIII's total destruction of the church and cloister since he needed **a royal guesthouse** halfway between Dover and Rochester. Account books remain showing the court's rapid adaptation to house Anne of Cleves. Between October and December 1539 300 builders worked round the clock to create the King's and Queen's apartments linked by the abbot's old chapel, drying out the plaster with candles and charcoal braziers. In the event, Anne stayed here only one night.

The royal palace was used occasionally, for instance during Queen Elizabeth I's three-day visit in 1574 for her fortieth birthday, by Charles I and Henrietta Maria on their honeymoon and by Charles II on his return in 1660. Mostly it was let to noble courtiers like Lord Wootton who occupied it from 1612, employing John Tradescant the elder to lay out splendid gardens over the abbey ruins. His wife Lady Margaret Wootton stored her firewood on the Mulberry Tree Common outside the gate, despite the frequent heavy fines of the local manor court and has triumphantly left her name behind on today's Green. She showed off the gardens to visitors like Captain Hammond in the 1630s. He told of a lake with Charon, his boat and dogs, surrounded by a set of 'watery nymphs', one 'disarmed by the right steady hand of his Majesty King Charles on the occasion of his marriage'. What story lies behind this episode?

After Lady Margaret's daughter had married into the Roman Catholic Hales family, the palace gradually fell into disrepair until by 1800 they had successively sold off land in Longport for the new courthouse, prison and hospital. The rest became a brewery and beer garden with skittles,

Butterfield Library. The Puginesque porch was a new construction since the Abbot's and Henry VIII's porch had been at the other end of the Great Hall opposite Fyndon Gate.

tennis and archery, cockfights above the gate and tightrope dancing or balloon ascents in the courtyard.

A new chapter opened in 1841 when the young MP James Beresford Hope, disgusted by the sad decline of England's first Christian abbey in a pagan country, bought the court for 2,000 guineas. Through a mutual friend he was eventually persuaded to found **a missionary college** there by Bishop Broughton, an old boy of the King's School and first bishop of Australia. William Butterfield, a disciple of Pugin, won his first important commission to adapt the buildings as a college in three years by St Peter's day 1848, the 1250th anniversary of the consecration of the first abbey. Described as 'a volcano of constricted passion' this self-taught son of a London chemist worked non-stop on every detail down to the kitchen chairs. He turned the great hall of abbots and kings into the library with a new south porch and workshops below for the trainee missionaries to learn carpentry. The library's clear windows gave the students a view of their predecessors' ruins on which excavations started as funds allowed. Butterfield's students' wing replaced Henry VIII's north wall with its surviving Tudor gate. It was built to Pugin's principles with steep pitched roofs and lavish use of tiles and flint. He made a double chapel from a gateway; in the lower one are recorded the deaths of missionaries in far-flung parts and of native converts dying here of British 'flu. Butterfield would go on with Hope's patronage to design All Saints, Margaret Street, Rugby School Chapel and Keble College, Oxford, in high Victorian Gothic style.

Christ Church University Chapel. This view from the St Augustine's Abbey ruins shows how the modern university like the Victorian missionary college before it remains conscious of its medieval traditions of building and scholarship.

The original abbey property, laboriously reunited by 1939, is now once again divided between Canterbury Christ Church University, the English Heritage site and the King's School who own the college buildings. They can be appreciated through the Fyndon Gate.

Canterbury Christ Church University

In September 1960 Dr Frederick Mason, fresh from the new University of Malaysia, arrived as the first principal of the first Church of England teacher training college since the war. His brief was to open the college to students within two years. The North Holmes site, part of St Augustine's college foundation, was acquired in two stages since it had been split between a malt house, orchards and the north holme, a deer park created for the royal palace which is pictured in a map of 1640. The core of the site was the outer domestic court created in Fyndon's day to the north of the abbey by absorbing the lane which once separated it from the craftsmen's village. The lane now exists again between Henry VIII's Tudor gate and the university campus.

In their haste and in days before prior archaeology was obligatory the college commissioned no below ground investigations in 1960. Expansion to bursting point has followed so swiftly that now piecemeal digs ahead of new buildings have allowed a gradual picture to emerge, akin to the Green Court at the cathedral priory. Foundations of buildings for the cellarer, baker and

Cemetery Gate. The monks, tenacious of their rights, often disputed with the city. A mayor once broke into the prison here to release a citizeness from their jurisdiction.

brewer and of a big kiln or malt house have been found round a gravelled courtyard and also traces of the infirmary to the east.

The first students began their courses in St Martin's Priory but moved on site in their second year. By 1964 hall, refectory, library and essential residential and teaching blocks had arisen. The striking chapel with its pointed roof was the focal point, visible from the Abbey ruins where education had first begun in the seventh century.

After 1972 teacher training became but one part of a diverse range of degree, professional and bridging courses offered to over 5,000 students, many of them mature or part-time. Today, 14,000 students study in what has become by stages a fully autonomous university. Three more campuses have been founded at Broadstairs, Chatham and Tunbridge Wells. Music and Humanities flourish alongside teacher, police, health and social care courses.

Like the King's School on its ex-monastic site, the university has had to spread into other buildings all over the city. Many organisations base vacation courses or visits at Christ Church which makes an excellent springboard for exploring Canterbury.

Walking up Monastery Street past the Butterfield buildings you reach the **Cemetery Gate** of 1391 on your left and Church Street St Paul's on your right. You stand here on the Roman road from Richborough Fort, their landing place. Soldiers, 30 kg packs on their backs, could march on this same road to Chester at twenty-five miles a day. Looking right, you can see where Burgate was once the Roman and Saxon main gate into the city. For centuries the public right of way to the Abbey's lay burial ground retained the Roman road line. The gate is not decorated

The Old Hospital This view shows the width of the monks' Longport market. The hospital was built over the probable burial site of Ethelbert and Bertha. (Canterbury Royal Museum & Art Gallery Copyright reserved 2007 ©)

showpiece like the Fyndon Gate but is full of Roman brick and other rubble from the original Roman cemetery over which the Abbey was built. The gate was converted into a house in the 1800s and is now home to King's School girls.

St Paul's Church was heavily Victorianised by Sir GG Scott in 1856 but its northern arcade and some thirteenth-century glass were probably the donation of its rector, Master Hamon Doge, in 1264. This busy city and church lawyer founded a chantry in the chapel of his own house in the Abbey's New Street leading to their leper hospital of St Lawrence. It is now called Lower Chantry Lane and halfway along the Chinese take-away occupies Doge's Chantry. He was eventually buried near his great friend the abbot leaving two valuable books to the Abbey.

A later churchwarden at St Paul's was the quarrelsome tailor James Chilton. With his wife and daughter he emigrated in the *Mayflower* in 1620 and was the twenty-fourth signatory of the Mayflower Compact, forming the Civil Body Politick which first planted democratic principles in New England. Young Mary Chilton survived the first bitter winter when both parents died and eventually married John Winslow, a founding father of Boston, and died in 1679.

A dog-leg here, as in Palace Street, was created when the monks extended their precinct. It leads into the wide **Longport**, the Abbey's long open market outside the city walls. Many disputes over tolls and jurisdiction pepper the records; the mayor once led a party to storm the monks' prison in the Cemetery Gate to release a Canterbury citizeness. Seventy burgesses lived in Longport when Domesday Book was compiled.

On the corner stands the cast-iron water outlet supplied by Sir John Hales in 1733 which remained in use until the 1900s. The wall beside it is medieval but the chequered wall of Tradescant's King's Garden was created out of demolition rubble. The rather forbidding brick façade of English Heritage's Visitor Centre was built in 1997 for the 1400th anniversary of

John and Ann Smith Almshouses. Unlike the similar Maynard and Cotton Hospital this row has no chapel. Inmates attended St Paul's Church to which the Smiths attached apprenticeship grants.

St Augustine's mission. Here are displayed the best fruits of over a century of excavations and excellent audio-guides at several levels make sense out of this complex Abbey site.

For 150 years the buildings of the **Kent and Canterbury Hospital** stood here. A meeting of clergy and gentry in September 1790 at the King's Head decided that East Kent needed a hospital. By December they had bought three acres from Sir Edward Hales who brought water to the site; by January plans were ready and the builder contracted. In April 1793 the hospital board opened this triumph of speed and efficiency offering twenty-four beds, four being reserved for accidents. Mrs Ann King the Matron, on 15 guineas a year, presided over two nurses and a porter, working with the apothecary, Mr Scudamore, on 30 guineas, who also ran an out-patients dispensary. They kept the drugs in a cupboard by the kitchen fire. Physicians and surgeons gave their services free; of their sixty-five patients in their first year, nineteen were cured, fourteen were relieved and four died. After the Kent and Canterbury Hospital moved to its present site in 1937 the buildings served until 1960 as a technical college and two schools and were demolished in 1972. The brick building facing up Longport is in fact a row of timber-framed cottages given a brick face-lift and converted into doctors' houses.

The large surface car park was the site of a primary school and cottages destroyed in the blitz of June 1942. Also damaged were the **Cooper Almshouses** across Lower Chantry Lane. Founded in 1900 for the ex-employees of a local firm the six cottages are but one of an amazing collection of eight continuing almshouses some dating back to 1084. By combining with a parish charity of 1711 Cooper Almshouses were handsomely restored in 1991. Further up Longport lies their neighbour **John and Ann Smith Almshouses** with their Flemish gables dated 1657. This Hornsey couple gave £1,500 for eight cottages in thank offering for the gift of a son after twenty years and four months of childless marriage. Now turned to back on to the traffic, four double units continue to provide this charity.

The Old Courthouse. Christ Church University's sensitive addition and adaptation have preserved this interesting building. Rapid expansion has outgrown the site of the 1960s Training College.

Continuing beyond the English Heritage building the mound on the left once supported the Abbey's bell tower. In the roadway beside it stood a tollgate, the outer boundary defence of the city like St Sepulchre's Bar on the old Dover Road. Hence beyond this boundary in 1808 a new **County Courthouse** was built by George Byfield to replace the old Sessions House near the castle. Its iron railings with their bundles of *fasces* were to symbolise the state's right to punish and execute. The court was once crowned with plaster allegorical figures and still bears a *fasces* crossed with a pole bearing a cap of liberty, since during the Napoleonic Wars we boasted of being alone in our combination of order with liberty; it is perhaps only a ceremonial cap of maintenance. The building has now been adapted as part of Christ Church University. An underground passage linked the courthouse to the neighbouring contemporary **prison**. At the time it was a 'panopticon', a model of modernity on Jeremy Bentham's principles. Being circular, the warders could supervise the seven categories of segregated prisoners, divided into 'decent and quiet first offenders', similar groups of 'old lags', 'decent and dissolute females', and 'thoroughbred housebreakers'. Made obsolete in 1920 it was reused in the war and since then has become over-full with prisoners doubled in cells originally intended for one.

Barton Court Grammar School opposite was for centuries the home farm, barns and manor court of St Augustine's Abbey. The pond, visible from the road, was the monks' fishpond, drained by Wat Tyler's rebels in 1381. The farm stretched from this Sandwich Road to the Old Dover Road; its manor court lasted until 1952. The elegant house of 1750 with its Venetian window and rusticated door has a first floor supported on an old ship's keel with its original rib-

Barton Court. William Hougham's money derived from his grandfather's trade with the Indies. The house he built in 1750 was already old-fashioned, in Queen Anne style.

holes marked in Roman numerals; all new oak at that time was earmarked for the Navy. I was privileged to teach history there for twelve years from its eighteenth-century dining room. Eight Victorian Chesshyre girls would skate with officers on the pond; seven daughters of General Russell who fought in the Zulu War maintained the farm until the war. It therefore fittingly housed the Girls' Technical School in the post-war years. After the blitz of 1942 the first telegram received in the city was from Kew Gardens enquiring the fate of a gingko tree in the grounds now flourishing at 250-years-old and 70ft tall.

You can return to the city centre in ten minutes either by Ivy Lane with its finely-restored hall house or by Lower Chantry Lane to the **New Dover Road.** This turnpiked road for the Dover mail coaches which connected with packet boats for France came into its own after St George's Gate came down in 1801. Traffic to the August race meeting on Barham Downs produced half the annual tolls. Although the north side was heavily bombed in 1942, Regency features remain in some of the offices on the south side. Despite bomb damage one of the two rival cinemas of 1933 still operates as Canterbury city's only cinema while the Marlowe Theatre occupies the other.

Beyond the traffic lights Victorian worthies built their villas in spacious grounds. Some have become hotels, most notably the extravagance of 'Abbots Barton', built by a disreputable Edwardian mayor. Many old gardens are now infilled or are the site of a new estate.

I hope the hotels, 'B and Bs' and Youth Hostel here will enable readers to spend longer than the usual day trip to explore the hidden wonders of a great city or to enjoy the Canterbury Festival in October.

Further Reading

The Cathedral

Recent books include:-
2004 A revised edition of the definitive work *A History of Canterbury Cathedral*, Collinson P., Ramsay N. and Sparks M. (OUP)
2004 *The Stained Glass of Canterbury Cathedral* Michael M. and Strobl S. (Scala Publishers)
2006 A reissue of the first and ground-breaking *Architectural History of Canterbury Cathedral* Willis R. 1845 (Tiger of the Stripe)
2007 *Canterbury Cathedral Precincts, a historical survey* Sparks M. (Dean and Chapter of Canterbury)
It is worth surfing the net to find:-
1986 *New Bell's Cathedral Guide* Ingram Hill D. (Bell)

Archbishops

2006 *The Archbishops of Canterbury* Maxwell-Scott P.G. (NPI Media Group)
1999 *St Augustine of Canterbury* Gameson R. (Cathedral Sources)
1986 *Thomas Becket* Barlow F. (Weidenfeld and Nicolson)
1999 *Thomas Becket – his last days* Urry W. ed. Rowe P. (Sutton Publishing)

Canterbury City

For photography and comment on the city before, during and after the Blitz of 1942:-
2006 *Canterbury's Lost Heritage* Crampton P. (Sutton Publishing)
2002 *Canterbury 1945-75 (Images of England)* Crampton P. (NPI Media Group)
Other titles by Paul Crampton are *Canterbury after the Blitz* and *Canterbury – the Buddleia Years* (Meresborough Books via the internet)
2002 *A Century of Canterbury* Butler D., has vintage photographs (Sutton Publishing)
2002 *Canterbury: 2000 years of History* (2nd edition) Lyle M. (Tempus). This is my archaeological history of the city.
Canterbury Archaeological Trust Ltd. publications are listed at www.canterburytrust.co.uk
The Trust has also produced *Roman Canterbury* and *A Journey into Mediaeval Canterbury*, both by Harmsworth A. and Green M. – best-sellers designed for school visits.

General

1985 *Drama in the Cathedral* Pickering K., covers Festival plays (Churchman Publishing)
1990 *From Vision to Reality* Martin G., is the early history of the University of Kent at Canterbury who publish it.
1997 *St Augustine's Abbey* Gem R. (English Heritage, available on site)

1991 *The Canterbury-Whitstable Railway* Hart B. (Wild Swan)
1983 *North-East and East Kent* Newman J. (Buildings of England – Penguin)
1984 *The Jews of Canterbury* Cohn-Sherbok D. (Yorick Books)
1995 *The Quest for Becket's Bones* Butler J. (Yale)
Some locally-produced booklets can be found at the Visitor Information Centre:-
Canterbury's Great Tycoon (James Simmons) Panton F.
The Ancient Almshouses and Hospitals of Canterbury Ingram Hill D. (reissued)
The Cradle of English Christianity and St Martin's Church Taylor M.
The Greyfriars of Canterbury Taylor M.

Literary

Chaucer's *Canterbury Tales* and Marlowe's *Plays* are in Penguin Classics.
2004 *The World of Christopher Marlowe* Riggs D. (Faber)
1990 *Written City* Brown P., Hutchinson S. and Irwin M. (Yorick Books) is a literary guide from Chaucer to Virginia Woolf.

The Kentish Context

2004 *An Historical Atlas of Kent* Lawson T. and Killingray D. (Phillimore) contains much Canterbury material
1966 *The Community of Kent and the Great Rebellion* Everitt A.M. (Leicester UP gives a vivid account of Civil War Canterbury.

Other local titles published by The History Press

Canterbury 2000 Years of History
MARJORIE LYLE

This work uses the various archaeological discoveries at Canterbury to show how the city's buildings, the Roman remains, Saxon churches, Norman Cathedral, inns and medieval houses are linked to the city's history. It will appeal to locals and visitors alike.

978 7524 1948 0

The Kent Downs
DAN TUSON

Nestled in the heart of the county, sparsely settled and largely untouched by modern-age pressures, the Kent Downs are home to some of the most enchanting countryside in England. This book unravels the history of the area's settlement and colonisation, the inspiration it has given to poets, artists and authors, and the legacy of its natural treasures; the rare and the commonplace; the peculiar and unique; the mysterious and the haunting.

978 0 7524 4405 5

Whitstable Then & Now
MICK GLOVER

Highlighting some wonderful comparisons, this unique collection of over eighty-five pairs of images takes a nostalgic look back at life as it once was in Whitstable, including the early influence of the railways and the bustling oyster markets for which the town is famous. *Whitstable Then & Now* will appeal to anyone interested in the heritage of this fascinating town and its surrounding communities over the past 100 years.

978 0 7524 3639 5

Old Kent Inns
DONALD STUART

The old inns of Kent have had a rich history since the first pilgrims came to Canterbury. They have been used as a hide-out by smugglers, highwaymen and deserters, seen the Civil Wars, the era of Napoleon and the bombing raids of the Second World War. Containing more than ninety photographs, this fascinating book tells of spy-holes and smugglers, murders and hangings, of escaped convicts and Siamese twins, phantom ships, hidden tunnels, hiding places and bodies bricked into walls.

978 0 7524 3959 4

If you are interested in purchasing other books published by The History Press, or in case you have difficulty finding any of our books in your local bookshop, you can also place orders directly through our website

www.thehistorypress.co.uk